JAMES COMEY

ABSOLUTELY NO LOYALTY

BY ME FOLKS...

ELLIOTT LEW GRIFFIN

AKA

THE MAKE AMERICA AMAZING GUY

JAMES COMEY

ABSOLUTELY NO LOYALTY

By: Elliott Lew Griffin

DISCOVERY CONSIST OF:

SEEING WHAT EVERYONE ELSE IS SEEING AND THINKING OUTSIDE THE BOX!

-Elliott Lew Griffin

OR IN THIS CASE IT'S THE TRUTH

AND I'M SORRY (NOT SORRY) JAMES COMEY

IT HAS FINALLY CAUGHT UP TO YOU...

WOW!

LONG TIME COMING HUH?

JAMES COMEY

ABSOLUTELY NO LOYALTY

By: Elliott Lew Griffin

THEN HE'S WRITING A BOOK CALLED:

JAMES COMEY
SAVING JUSTICE

AND NOW I'M WRITING ANOTHER BOOK CALLED:

JAMES COMEY

MURDERED JUSTICE

WHY?

BECAUSE JAMES COMEY MURDERED JUSTICE

THAT'S WHY

AND YET

ANOTHER PRIME EXAMPLE OF GOOD COP GONE BAD

OR WAS HE EVER?

I DON'T KNOW!

ALL I CAN SAY AT THIS POINT IS STAY TUNED YOUR READING...

JAMES COMEY - ABSOLUTELY NO LOYALTY!

MOM-

"WE HAVE A SITUATION"

BREAKING NEWS

BREAKING NEWS

JAMES COMEY

OFFICIALLY, A LIAR AND A LEAKER!

JAMES COMEY

OFFICIALLY, A LIAR AND A LEAKER!

JAMES COMEY

ABSOLUTELY NO LOYALTY

By: Elliott Lew Griffin

AWW MAN
WHAT COMES NEXT RIGHT?

TRUMP:

"COMEY'S A LIAR AND A LEAKER"

AND

(THE DEMOCRATS CAN KEEP HIM)

THE DEMOCRATS:

"COMEY'S A LIAR AND A LEAKER"

AND

(WE DON'T WANT HIM EITHER)

JAMES COMEY

ABSOLUTELY NO LOYALTY

By: Elliott Lew Griffin

TRUMP:

(YES, YOU DO)

EDITED BY ME FOLKS-

ELLIOTT LEW GRIFFIN!

NO RIGHTS RESERVED

THAT SHOULD TELL YOU SOMETHING

JAMES COMEY

ABSOLUTELY NO LOYALTY

By: Elliott Lew Griffin

IT'S A MUST READ...

JAMES COMEY

ABSOLUTELY NO LOYALTY

By: Elliott Lew Griffin

OR NOT!!!

HEY: SO FAR SO GOOD RIGHT?

JAMES COMEY

ABSOLUTELY NO LOYALTY

By: Elliott Lew Griffin

YEAH: YOU SHOULD HAVE STOPPED AT THE LAST PAGE

HOWEVER, TO SAY THE LEAST:

IT'S A MUST READ!!!

IT'S A MUST-READ FOLKS...

JAMES COMEY

ABSOLUTELY NO LOYALTY

By: Elliott Lew Griffin

A MUST-READ FOLKS...

JAMES COMEY

ABSOLUTELY NO LOYALTY

By: Elliott Lew Griffin

READ FOLKS....

JAMES COMEY

ABSOLUTELY NO LOYALTY

By: Elliott Lew Griffin

FOLKSSS...

JAMES COMEY

ABSOLUTELY NO LOYALTY

By: Elliott Lew Griffin

HEY WHAT CAN I SAY:

IF THERE'S A BOOK YOU REALLY WANT TO READ BUT IT HASN'T BEEN WRITTEN YET, THEN YOU MUST WRITE IT!!

-TONI MORRISON

WELL FOLKS:

THIS IS WHAT I CAME UP WITH?

AND TO SAY THE VERY LEAST...

YOU TOO MUST WANT TO READ IT!

SO:

ARE YOU READY???

ARE YOU READY???

THEN TURN THE PAGE FOLKS.....

WHAT ARE YOU WAITING FOR???

OMG

LET'S GOOOOO!!!

JAMES COMEY

ABSOLUTELY NO LOYALTY

By: Elliott Lew Griffin

OH, NEXT PAGE - NEXT PAGE FOLKS

ONE MORE – WE'RE WORKING ON IT...

WE'RE WORKING ON IT FOLKS

OMG

DOES THIS COUNT AS ANOTHER ONE?

I KNOW - I KNOW - WE'RE GOING TO GET IT RIGHT

WE'RE TRYING - WE'RE TRYING FOLKS

JAMES COMEY

ABSOLUTELY NO LOYALTY

By: Elliott Lew Griffin

WAS THAT LAST PAGE JUST BLANK???

I DON'T KNOW WHY THEY KEEP DOING THIS TO YOU FOLKS...

LET ME CHECK IT OUT-LET ME CHECK IT OUT FOR YOU FOLKS

I'LL TELL YOU WHAT-I'LL TELL YOU WHAT THOUGH...

IF JAMES COMEY DID HAVE A HIGHER LOYALTY TO US THE AMERICAN PEOPLE......

THEN I WOULD HATE TO SEE WHAT HIS LOWER LOYALTY LOOKED LIKE, FORREAL!

JUST THINK??

HIS HIGHER LOYALTY - WAS ALREADY ABSOLUTELY NO LOYALTY

SO, YOU DO THE MATH BECAUSE I ALREADY DONE IT...

AND YOU KNOW WHAT IT EQUATES TOO?

JAMES COMEY

ABSOLUTELY NO LOYALTY

OMG
A MUST READ!!!

HOWEVER:

THESE NEXT FEW PAGES ARE ABOUT A SERIOUS ISSUE THAT I WOULD LIKE TO SHED LIGHT ON WITH THIS BOOK SO PLEASE BARE WITH ME AND LISTEN UP REAL CLOSE.... (IT'S DISTURBING TO U.S.)

-THANK YOU!

JAMES COMEY

ABSOLUTELY NO LOYALTY

By: Elliott Lew Griffin

NEXT PAGE – NEXT PAGE PLEASE

THE UNITED STATES LEADS WORLD IN INCARCERATING WOMEN!!!

According to a 2017 report by Prison Policy Initiative, individual states of the U.S. along with the federal government lead the world in putting women behind bars. Women in the U.S. only represent 5% of the world's female population but account for nearly 30% of the world's in prison women population. Across the globe the 25 jurisdictions with the highest rate of incarcerated women are all American states.

Approximately 206,000 women are currently confined in prisons or jails across America. The crazy part is America jails women at four times the percentage rate of Russia, and America blames Russia for a lot of things. America also blames China for a lot of things but America jails women at twice the percentage rate of China, and they're communist. They say Thailand is the first non-U.S. state that incarcerates more women at #26 on the list. Therefore, 25 out of our 50

JAMES COMEY

ABSOLUTELY NO LOYALTY

By: Elliott Lew Griffin

U.S. states incarcerates more women than any other industrialized country in the world.

The United States also incarcerate women 8 to 25 times higher than some of our closest allies. According to a recent study the U.S. incarceration rate is 127 per 100,000 women while other allied countries such as the UK rate is only 13 per 100,000; Canada is 11 per 100,000; France which just had a state dinner with Trump is 6 per 100,000; and Denmark's the lowest with five per 100,000. But again, we are 127 per 100,000.

In the United States women have become the most fastest growing segment of the incarcerated population. The state of Illinois's incarceration rate is on par with the entire country of El Salvador. Which many women are currently escaping with this new wave of caravanning immigrants currently traveling through Mexico to get to the United States. I mean we sit here every day and talk about the civil wars and brutal regimes of El Salvador, then I would hate to say what our state government in Illinois's is like? Isn't that where Chicago is?? Where all those shootings occur every night???

Another example that shocked me the most was when they said the state of New Hampshire is on par with the entire country of Russia in locking up women and this is a country that America has been claiming is the worst of the worst in recent years. From everything to annexing Crimea and perpetuating the Russian hoax. You do remember the Russian hoax right folks? But again, if America incarcerates women at four times the amount of Russia then what does that say about us in the U.S. really?

They also report that the state of New York is on par with incarcerating more women than the country of Rwanda. Rhode Island is among the lowest incarceration states for women but it's still twice that of Portugal, and they even estimated that if Rhode Island were an entire country that it would still ranked #15 on the list of incarcerated women all around the world. Small ass Rhode Island number 15 on the list of incarcerating women around the world, how sad!

Like they say perhaps the most troubling finding about women's incarceration is how little progress states have made in curbing its growth. It has gotten even more out of control. They have reported in states like Michigan that woman imprisonment grew 30% just between 2009 to 2015. During the same time frame the state of Texas added over 1100 women to its prison system. The state of Idaho recently refilled half of its prison beds it emptied from its men's population by adding 25% more women to its prison.

Thus, while states like California, New York and New Jersey are the few states that have reversed course and begun sending woman home; Other states continue to widen the net by criminalizing women's response to gender based abuse and discrimination. These policies have led to mandatory and dual arrest for women fighting back against domestic violence and they have even increased the criminalization of school age girl's misbehavior.

Which many of their offenses include running away for survival, and or turning to sex work to put food on the table. Not to mention a vast majority of these sex working women were abused and molested as kids and therefore have real mental health issues underlining their drug addictions and everything else in between.

JAMES COMEY

ABSOLUTELY NO LOYALTY

By: Elliott Lew Griffin

Like one girl reported and I'm not going to mention her name, but she said in my case my trauma as a kid was never acknowledged and the phrase "child sex trafficking survivor" was never used. She was molested as a kid, abused as a teen, and incarcerated as an adult because she never could get the real mental health treatment she needed to overcome the mistreatment she endured while growing up as a kid here in America.

To say the least, there are many more like her that have turned to drug use to mask their underlining mental health issues of the traumatic experiences they've endured growing up and it is their addictions I believe that have driven women's prison growth in America. That and corrupt politicians that don't care about none of the above. Like the lady said, "child sex trafficking survivor was never even mentioned in my case", and I wouldn't even want to speak it upon them, but I'm fairly sure molestation, rape and forced trafficking wasn't either.

Studies show that more than 1 million women are on probation and another 123,000 or so are on parole. Another study revealed that 60% of women in jail have not been

41

convicted of a crime and are awaiting trial. The disproportionality large percentage of non-convicted women in jail is because females have lower income than incarcerated males and therefore it's harder from them to afford bail. Other times women are forced into sex trafficking where the actual trafficker gets mostly all the money and when these women are captured by authorities, they are left to face the legal ramifications of their actions on their own.

I would like to shed light on this issue in this book because this issue should be a growing concern on everyone's heart and mind. I say that because I had watched this show called intervention and the episode, I watched was about a young girl who was raped and after that she was never the same. Her life was ruined. She had turned to drugs to help mask her emotional trauma and after that the drugs took over. She couldn't control either one anymore, her mental health issues or her drug addiction. She had turned to sex work to supply her drug addiction. Then of course everyone knows what happens after that. Jail, prison, or worse death. They say women's incarceration demands more attention because of these distinct issues that many little girls growing up into women have faced.

JAMES COMEY

ABSOLUTELY NO LOYALTY

By: Elliott Lew Griffin

And it sad because the judicial system has completely failed these women that are battling these dual diagnostic issues. Now I know in the last year we have talked a lot about the #METOO movement, and I would just like to call on those other women to say, please don't forget about these other women as well. They have a story to tell and they should be heard. They have a name and it should be read as well. They have a real need for help that should be addressed. I just hope that women will hear this and help them too.

I don't know, I don't have an end all solution to the problem at this time, but it is my greatest hope that bringing awareness on this issue here may at least get it some attention. I know somewhere there is help, we just must think outside the box to find it. As far as this James Comey book goes, I would like to apologize now. I got to the end of writing this book and thought about what a great opportunity I've missed to shine the light on the corrupt judicial system that I have come to know. I'm going to be forthcoming to say that I am incarcerated and have been wrongfully incarcerated for the past 15 years. I beat up a guy that was trying to steal my car trailer and even as a first-time offender I got life in prison. (Life in prison for stopping a thief

JAMES COMEY

ABSOLUTELY NO LOYALTY

By: Elliott Lew Griffin

that was stealing my property).(Yeah, okay...freaking Do Nothing Demoncrats)   Honestly, I don't like to talk about it because I always thought I could handle it on my own, but as the days turn to months and the months into years, I've realized that the judicial system is so corrupt and that it's going to take a freaking miracle worker to fix it. I actually just found out about self-publishing books on Amazon, so I wrote the March for Our Lives book which I felt came out pretty good. As far as this Comey book I just wrote it for the idea on the cover and when I got towards the end of it, I thought about how I should have written it for the message. For that I'm sorry .... The more I think about it, this was really a missed opportunity given the fact that I know just the cover of this book may draw some kind of media attention and that's why I went back and at least included this piece in here now.

I don't have the time, or energy, nor the resources to rewrite this entire book, but where a door closes a window opens up and all of this made me think about writing another book titled: "Mass Incarceration" "The unmasking of mass incarceration in America". Please see attached. In that book I aim to talk about my 15 years of experience with dealing with the corrupt judicial

44

system and what we can do to fix it. I have a lot of ideas/answers to do so. I also want to open up the dialogue, so that our criminal justice system is not only working for the people in society, but for all those affected by it as well, especially the woman we're talking about here today. I've come to find out by sitting in groups and listen to a lot of people talk that everyone has a story and it's a shame that many of them will never be heard.

Well I Hope that by just acknowledging it here in this book that we have a mass growing problem with women incarceration here in America, that this is a step in the right direction. And what we do about it going forward is a question remained to be seen. I could tell you what? The Demoncrats aren't the answer to fixing it because they're behind it The Repulsicans aren't the answer to fix it because they're behind it too. So, what is the answer, stay tuned folks your goanna finds out real fast, but hey with this book we want to shine light on our mass growing women's incarceration problem Today. Especially since most of these women are real trauma victims that are in need of help and a lot of TLC, not mass incarceration. And definitely not to be treated like ****.

45

JAMES COMEY

ABSOLUTELY NO LOYALTY

By: Elliott Lew Griffin

MASS INCARCERATION

"THE UNMASKING OF MASS INCARCERATION IN AMERICA"

NOT FOR THE FEINT OF HEARTS

IT'S REALLY THAT BAD FOLKS!!

OMG

A MUST READ!!!

JAMES COMEY

ABSOLUTELY NO LOYALTY

By: Elliott Lew Griffin

PLEASE DON'T ACT LIKE YOU DON'T KNOW

TO BE CONTINUED...

WELL WITHOUT FURTHER A DO I PRESENT TO YOU...

JAMES

COMEY

ABSOLUTELY
NO
LOYALTY

YOU ASKED

FOR IT

AND WHO DELIVERED ???

JAMES COMEY

ABSOLUTELY NO LOYALTY

By: Elliott Lew Griffin

AGAIN!

ELLIOTT

LEW

GRIFFIN

THE

MAKE

AMERICA

AMAZING

GUY

JAMES COMEY

ABSOLUTELY NO LOYALTY

By: Elliott Lew Griffin

THIS BOOK IS WRITTEN TO EXPOSE JAMES COMEY...

FOR WHO HE REALLY IS???

AND I'M PRETTY SURE YOU SAW THAT ON THE COVER

"JAMES COMEY – ABSOLUTELY NO LOYALTY"

LIKE THEY SAY:

A LIE CAN BE HALFWAY AROUND THE WORLD

BEFORE THE TRUTH HAS GOT IT'S BOOTS ON

-PROVERB

WELL COMEY:

THE TRUTH HAS GOT IT'S BOOTS ON

AND NOW IT'S COMING FOR YOU

JAMES COMEY

ABSOLUTELY NO LOYALTY

By: Elliott Lew Griffin

WE KNOW WHAT YOU DID LAST SUMMER COMEY!

DON'T RUN NOW:

TRUTH IS ON THE MARCH AND

NOTHING CAN STOP IT NOW...

IT'S COMING FOR YOU COMEY – IT'S COMING FOR YOU

LIKE I SAY:

PEOPLE MAY FALL FOR A LIE WHEN THEY DON'T KNOW THE TRUTH

BUT WHEN THEY LEARN THE TRUTH, THEY WILL KNOW 100% THAT YOU LIED

AND THAT'S WHY WE CREATED THE COVER RIGHT?

JAMES COMEY

ABSOLUTELY NO LOYALTY

I BET YOU:

EVEN WHEN JAMES COMEY SEE'S THE COVER...

HE'S GOING TO SAY: "AWE- THEY CAUGHT ME"

AND IT WOULD HAVE TO BE THAT GUY...

JAMES COMEY

ABSOLUTELY NO LOYALTY

By: Elliott Lew Griffin

.

THE MAKE AMERICA AMAZING GUY

AHHA JAMES COMEY – I GOT YOU TOO

OR BETTER YET...

YOU GOT YOURSELF RIGHT???

JUST STATING FACTS DUDE

SO, BACK UP OFF ME

JAMES COMEY

ABSOLUTELY NO LOYALTY

By: Elliott Lew Griffin

FACTS MATTER – FACTS MATTER
ABOUT AN FBI DIRECTOR THAT DISTORTED THEM
(RIGHT?)

YEAH OKAYYYYYY…
WE'RE GOING TO FIND OUT
COME SEPTEMBER 30TH, 2020??

JAMES COMEY

ABSOLUTELY NO LOYALTY

By: Elliott Lew Griffin

AND AS A MATTER OF FACT, WHERE WAS WE...

JAMES COMEY

ABSOLUTELY NO LOYALTY

By: Elliott Lew Griffin

OH
OMG

PROLOGUE

What more can I say other than we got another good one for you today folks. It's a real thriller about Slippery Shady James Comey, the worst FBI director in United States history. A real slimeball! I'm pretty sure you heard of him, come on, liar, top-secret FBI serial leaker yeah, we're talking about the same guy. Well then you already know this guy is all bad, all bad folks.

All I can say is don't listen to a word he says. He may tell you the truth about his name, it's James Comey Jr., but after that warning warning warning you're listening to him at your own risk. What more can I say you want to keep something confidential or a secret don't show it to him or tell it to him folks, he'll leak it.

I'll tell you what, by the time you're done reading this book you're going to be sitting there wondering why James Comey isn't locked up. Or two, your voice is going to be so hoarse from screaming lock him up lock him up that in the end you're going to be left standing there with your arms up and a Sean Hannity look on your face like are you guys really going to lock this guy up or what? Sean Hannity folks you know he be onto real corruption, real corruption. But seriously, it's unbelievable folks how these people get away with their corrupt scandals. We got to start holding them accountable or else they're going to keep doing it and getting away with it.

Anyhow you may want to buckle up and hold onto your seats cause you're in for a wild ride in reading about this guy. Like I say, what more can I say, nothing seems to amaze me these days. James Comey either. But please stay tuned folks your reading...

JAMES COMEY – ABSOLUTELY NO LOYALTY

JAMES COMEY

ABSOLUTELY NO LOYALTY

By: Elliott Lew Griffin

1

CHAPTER 1

JAMES COMEY
ABSOLUTELY NO LOYALTY

When I first saw James Comey's book, I instantly thought what a crock.... A higher loyalty, like, yeah right? If anything, it's a higher loyalty to the devil, especially since his half-truths, whole lies, lack of leadership, treasonous top secret FBI leaking and meddling in our 2016 presidential election clearly proved that he had absolutely no loyalty whatsoever to us the American people. I don't know who, what, when, where, how or why someone would pump Comey up to put that on this cover, except to assert that they must have already knew that he was going to start lying from the beginning.

Seriously, I would have thought that Comey's editor would have told him to change his title, but again they edited the book so I'm quite sure they knew he was lying from the beginning as well. To be honest I could see Comey's editor tell him to change the title and he respond... What for they already know that I'm lying. Why tell the truth now right probably laughing? (The joke

67

JAMES COMEY

ABSOLUTELY NO LOYALTY

By: Elliott Lew Griffin

that wasn't the joke right) Hint hint! I know if I had to ever judge Comey's book by its cover, I swear hands down I would vote that many scrolls in there he's lying. I'm serious, that's sad when we can't even get past the front cover of his book and all agree, he's already lying. Like what does it say "A Higher Loyalty" like yeah-yeah, he's lying. I know if anything, he should have titled it "I'm Sorry" or "I Really Didn't Know" and or "I HAD TRUMP DERANGE SYNDROME WHEN I DID IT" especially with all the lying, top secret (FBI) Leaking and Meddling in our 2016 election he did. #WOW

I honestly can't tell you what he's thinking, but if he was looking for 15 minutes of fame, I regret to inform him that in my view he's only getting 15 more minutes of shame. I know he's been getting paid off his book tour, but that money isn't going to save his butt from going to jail when our second special counsel gets ahold of his tail.

You know what? I haven't read his book, but then again, I'm not going to, what do I need to read his book for? To continuously be lied to. OMG why do I need to pay him to do that, if I wanted to see him continue to lie to me all I had to do turn on the news and watch all of his pathetic interviews. I heard that ABC had to edit five hours to get that one hour George Stephanopoulos interview and out of that whole hour the only time I felt I wasn't being lied too was when George Stephanopoulos was asking Comey the questions.

I guess if anyone enjoys being lied to, I would highly recommend they read James Comey's book "A higher loyalty". Like what everybody from the right to the left and everybody

JAMES COMEY

ABSOLUTELY NO LOYALTY

By: Elliott Lew Griffin

else in between knows that James Comey is a liar, James Comey is a serial leaker and that James Comey has absolutely no loyalty to the government and or us the American people and to say the least that's exactly why he's hated on both sides of the aisle. Yes, I guess he's not hated too much his book sold in the millions, but okayyyy.

Like what, I can't believe Comey wrote a book and cashed in on it. And with the American people too. If anything, I would have thought he would have sold it in Russia or something like that, because he did absolutely nothing for the American people, but a disservice. That's why I'm sitting here thinking wow, HOW COULD HE, and that's why I was glad when he got fired.

He sat up here and stole Confidential Documents from the FBI Building and then leaked them to his friend who in turn leaked them to the press.

Like I always say, why couldn't Comey just stand up there in the FBI BUILDING and say HEY I BELIEVE I HAVE INFORMATION THAT MORE LIKEY THAN NOT WOULD LEAD TO THE IMPEACHMENT OF THE PRESIDENT. (President Trump) But "NO" again he hid in the shadows and tried to do some lying leaky sneaky weasel move but got caught. (Caught committing crimes and the head guy of the FBI didn't go to jail).

And that's why it comes as no surprise that the number two guy went bad too.

Then, how can you not look at the title his book a higher loyalty and not conclude he was already lying. I'm sorry, I

JAMES COMEY

ABSOLUTELY NO LOYALTY

By: Elliott Lew Griffin

honestly can't get over the title period. To me he could have titled it anything other than that, but I guess that just proves my theory that anything he comes up with is a lie. (Man) I Swear I could come up with all kinds of titles that would sell James Comey. James Comey the serial leaker. James Comey the FBI fixer of the 2016 presidential election. How 'bout that one because he really blew it for Hillary Clinton at the end if she didn't do it to herself when becoming Crooked Hillary.

I mean what was Comey trying to do with his book defend his decisions. Does he know that there is not a micro Organism of inferences that could ever defend his position? Then what can he say we got wrong? We know he's a liar. He's already admitted to leaking and we know he abused his power to meddle in (our) 2016 presidential election for corrupt reasons? What more can we say other than he made our intelligence agencies in the world appear weak. James Comey, he reeks of stink. And the sad part is that's the truth. James Comey, he betrayed you and me. And my Mom too. (That bastard) She was voting for Hillary that year and that's the truth. Like for real, you think I'm playing, but this is a sad state to see that our number one guy in charge of the FBI was a leaker, an official admitted leaker. Then again like I said, it comes as no surprise that our number two guy Andrew McCabe went sour and I hate to say it, but that's what we get for failing to hold our number one guy James Comey accountable. Not to give him a million-dollar book tour and a bunch of interviews. Just think, why wouldn't McCabe want to follow in those shoes? (Well I guess he already did huh?) I guess it's only a matter of time until he does his million-dollar book tour. (Man) maybe I'll get one huh? James Comey folks (Absolutely No Loyalty) Now I even

JAMES COMEY

ABSOLUTELY NO LOYALTY

By: Elliott Lew Griffin

heard Peter struck was on his way doing a book tour about some book that he wrote and the statements he made and everybody know about him and what he told his then FBI girlfriend that he was sleeping with (Why they were both just sneaking around violating FBI protocol). (Man) I guess everybody was just lying cheating sneaking and doing weasel moves. I guess everybody was violating FBI protocol, right?

I mean look at what is going around? They had all kinds of scandals going on and now he's writing a book and doing a book tour. Yeah okay…. (And I'm not against his FBI Romance because a lot of people meet at work, but folks be man or women enough to step up and tell the truth, especially as an FBI agent. I mean come on. Shame the devil sometimes.

I mean he would be dumb not to continue to do a book tour, but this book does go right up there somewhere with OJ Simpson's book "If I Done It". Or "If I had a higher loyalty". To be fair I'm sitting here thinking do I have to write more, or can I just show you the front cover of this book and say hey look here you go. There it goes right there folks. You have it right there in front of you. James Comey - Absolutely No Loyalty. I mean really what do you want me to say hi how are you doing? What more can I say but the truth James Comey, all bad folks.

I could tell you, I really thought about ordering his book and make a serious response to it, but then I thought what more than this would I come up with, so I'm better off just saving my money, saving my mind and saving my time from reading his book. This I felt could also save you know some trees. Like I say, buying Comey's book would be insane. That's what I say not only would I be spending my hard earned money on garbage, or listening to more of his lies, but killing a tree in the process for a stupid James Comey book is my biggest problem.

We are already facing a global warming crisis and to kill another tree for Comey's book I deserve to be breathing bad oxygen. Why? Because I breathe the air that the carbon dioxide tree gives out. So, I breathe in oxygen and exhale carbon dioxide. The tree sucks in the carbon dioxide and gives out the oxygen I currently breathe, so yes, I'll be killing a tree that's keeping me alive to read James Comey's book in a global warming crisis. To be honest I'd rather save the tree to try to suck up some of the hot air carbon dioxide that Comey is currently spewing around. To say the least killing trees to print his book is killing our ecosystem. I mean really. How do we justify killing a tree, for a stupid lying James Comey read? Honestly, how can I take Comey's book seriously... when he's already lying to me on the front cover. The only thing he's probably told the truth about what's his name and the word (Lies) on the front cover, after that, I don't believe another word of it, especially when I know that a higher loyalty, truth and leadership is nowhere to be found in him.

I mean he may be right about his view of trump as a mob boss, but I tell you what? Trump's 100% right about viewing Comey as a slimeball. I mean Comey's out here trying to damage a lot of people's political career, but all this information is coming from a man that single handedly ruined his. I mean maybe Comey never cared about it to begin with, that's probably why he's

JAMES COMEY

ABSOLUTELY NO LOYALTY

By: Elliott Lew Griffin

never been candid in leaking information and probably been doing so since the beginning.

I always wondered how [he] got to the top and now I know? He lied his way all the way there.... The only problem is his lies eventually caught up with him, so now he's resorting to telling more lies in an attempt to throw discord over them all. What they say, if none is true then all spectacle? Yeah that's James Comey right now for sure? I guess we're watching the James Comey show. All I can say, is good thing it's only 15 minutes and not 30. To be honest after 16 minutes I might not never watch that news channel again. Like the heck with it, I guess Donald Trump is right about this one, it's all fake news folks. Fake news about fake people. Or it could be real news about fake people and that's why it always is fake.

Seriously, just the sound of Comey's book is a disgrace from a top American FBI official, but then again this is James Comey we're talking about, right? Then hey, just saying... I'm not too surprised at all to find that the Apple didn't roll too far from the tree again when we're talking about the number two guy right Andrew McCabe just got fired for doing the same thing. I guess birds of a feather do flock together. Now I'm sitting here wondering what his book would look like. What will his story be? What will Andrew McCabe's book tour look like or is he another James Comey lie his way all the way thru it.

The hilarious part will be if McCabe wrote a book ousting James Comey. I would laugh and buy it just for the cover. Andrew McCabe in a tell all book about James Comey. I wonder what it would look like. McCabe "I felt Comey was trying to run the FBI like a mob boss, but he really didn't know what he's doing. Try to copy the mob boss in Trump but you know what happened. Comey also told me that he made up the Russian story about trump being in that hotel room with prostitutes peeing on themselves just so he could sell more books."

I mean where are we at? Isn't that in his book? I mean this is all the stuff Comey produced. Comey also taught me it was OK to lie. I mean is what we're teaching our kids right now. The head FBI director of the FBI is lying. He's supposed to be counterintelligence and all his answers we're counter to our intelligence, and or an outright assault on our intelligence. Talking about counterintelligence right. Yeah, like I say, one thing for sure, we can't count on James Comey's intelligence. Why? Because the way he's lying I can't believe he has intelligence and or again he must think we don't. I mean as an FBI Director James Comey should be able to catch everybody lying in lies and what do we have here? We have us catching him in lies. We have us catching him admitting to doing wrong doings. And now he's doing a book tour. Yeah if you ask me, he should be doing a book tour from cell to cell. "Hey, I wrote a book you want to buy it". Other prisoners looking at him like, "you know we broke". And the one's that got money are looking at Comey like I'm not going to support you lying to me.

Hey what can I say, Comey taught me that watching his interviews. How to lie like an FBI director. All else fails tell them what they want to hear .... In this situation when it comes to Hillary, Comey alleges he made a mistake, but just look on the bright side "I know there's some evidence to impeach trump". And those are Comey's words, not mine.

Isn't that's part of the FBI model right, help them get the bigger fish and they'll let you off the hook every time. I guess Comey figures why stop the trend now. I will give him some credit for being smart enough to apply it on a mass scale. Seriously, that's what all of this sounds like to me, a bunch of imbeciles telling on each other to try to get rich and get themselves out of trouble. At least one thing we can say, Comey knows the tricks of the trade and currently employing them to use the Demoncrats like a fiddle because really aren't they the ones doing a book tour for him anyway.

He sold out Hillary Clinton during the 2016 presidential election and probably got paid for it and now he's trying to sell out Donald Trump with his book and getting paid for it. I see where the Russians get it from now, James Comey or better yet did Comey get this tactic from the Russians. First, it's alleged that the Russian sowed discord for trump and then after he won, they were alleged to have sowed discord against them. In this case, before the election Comey's thru discord against Hillary and after Trump won, he sold discord against him. You catch the drift?

I would say it's the perfect cover up. He sold out Hillary in 2016 and for that I'm willing to place a wager that Comey played a part in his wife and daughter attending the Women's March against Trumps inauguration. I bet you he was running around the house like a madman. Trump won and now we got to go marching in the streets to get him impeached. However, if you

JAMES COMEY

ABSOLUTELY NO LOYALTY

By: Elliott Lew Griffin

ask me, his wife and kid attending the women's march against trump was the perfect cover for selling out Hillary Clinton 11 days before the election. To say the least, I heard Demoncrats say for that reason Comey didn't sell out Hillary, he must be telling truth, it was a mistake.

This dude is alleged to be a super-duper double-crossing FBI agent and for that reason I can't believe a word Comey's says. I bet you that's how he rose to the top of the ranks playing people against each other. In law enforcement is called a ruse, where you lie to a person to get them to lie on another person or themselves. Then you continue to play on each of them until you get them both entangled. What is an FBI Director salary anyway 100 to 200,000 a year? Just think Comey scorns everyone on both sides and now getting paid from everyone on both sides to write about it? Am I missing something?

I mean let's look at it this way, we know he sold out both sides, so for that reason we know he didn't do it for a higher loyalty. That leaves me with the only other conclusion and that is he sold out both sides for "A Higher Royalty". And that's why I say folks his book should have been called "A Higher Royalty" and not "A Higher Loyalty". Especially since he's cashing in on it. I guess I got to make-up a salacious story about Trump too. Either him or Hillary, but maybe if I just stick to James Comey everybody seems to be against him right now.

They say, everybody complains about the same thing and in this case it's James Comey, but nothing ever gets done about it because everyone isn't tired at the same time. In that case all I have to do is wait for everyone to be mad at Comey and I might be able to cash in on this book at that time. Hey, it's not me, I'm using reason, logic, and common sense to try to psychoanalyze the mind of James Comey. He got paid for writing a book about Donald Trump when everybody was mad at him right, so if I use his psychoanalyzed mind state, like I just said I'll be right there too. I'm doing analyst on how James Comey used his FBI tactics to play the left and the right against each other and walk away with all of their money? Then I have watched him use his famous law enforcement tactics so he can scab from underneath all culpability by simply saying "I can't recall, or I don't remember?" And I'm surprised he hasn't used the third one "let me check my notes".

You know what, I was really appalled when I saw Comey an FBI director in his ABC interview claim he could not recall back to what he was thinking during the 2016 presidential election. Then when George Stephanopoulos was helping him out Comey would just go along with him, saying "I can't recall and that must have been what I was thinking?"

For real, on a serious note, Trump got it right and James Comey should be in jail. He's meddled in our 2016 presidential election twice as much as any Russian ever could. I don't know if his actions actually changed the outcome of the election, but the fact that he did it nonetheless is still a crime. They still can't say if the Russian trolls on social media had an effect, but that didn't stop Congress and trump from coming down with sanctions on Russia, right? So, what's the difference here again?

But now we have Comey sitting here getting paid millions of his book tour and there is still no investigation on him. He interfered with our 2016 presidential election hands down and if that's not enough for a second special counsel, then hey there's more. He clearly abused his FBI Director power to meddle in election. He's lied under oath to Congress. He admitted under oath to taking highly classified FBI secrets. He's violated many FBI rules and now he's trying to profit off all his crimes, so how is he still walking around on the streets instead of being jailed in some federal prison cell. I know if all of that isn't enough to get a second special counsel on Comey, then we got to start investigating the ones making decisions to say no to the special counsel because they should be jailed for obstruction of justice as well. That's why I say that we the people got to get rid of our crooked leaders in Congress because they should be holding these torps accountable. That goes for James Comey, Andrew McCabe, and everybody else in between firing him wasn't enough especially now that James Comey's cashing in on it. It's only a matter of time for McCabe to think he can do the same thing. Then like I said, Peter Strzok just did the same thing. Now if he's set to get millions off his book. Then like I said, what's going to stop the number 3 guy or the number 4 in the FBI from doing the exact same thing. Like I said whose next Lisa Page ousting Peter Strzok. Why work for 200 grand a year when I can screw the system, cash in on millions, and not go to jail for it. I can sell government secrets. I can sell lies. I can be Wells Fargo and cheat the people and not go to jail for it; write a book and get paid for it.

Well in the United States don't we have a law against People profiting off their crimes by writing books and movies about what they did and how they did it? And those laws don't apply

JAMES COMEY

ABSOLUTELY NO LOYALTY

By: Elliott Lew Griffin

here to James Comey's book? And that's why I say folks, James Comey Absolutely No Loyalty. Because that's what I keep talking about folks. What are we talking about James Comey's lying book tour, no jail? Peter Strzok new book, no jail and cashing in on it. And to boot, the public was actually eating this up like they love it, just saying. Like I say, no accountability will only bring about further destruction to our democracy. Did you hear that, or should I repeat that? "No accountability will only bring about further destruction to our democracy".

I tell you what, these two FBI Imposters, James Comey and Lacking Candor Andrew McCabe has totally ruined the FBI's credibility with this generation for an exceptionally long time. And I know that there are FBI officials that do an amazing job to keep us all safe, but when you have high ranking corruption scandals going on in between at the top, one can only think "what's really going on at the bottom?" Like I say if this type of behavior is going on at the top, then I would hate to see "what's going in between" and worse "at the bottom". Do you see where we're headed with that? If you have corruption and practically everything going on at the top, just imagine what's going on at the bottom. Then we look at the miss tips of the Marjory Stoneman Douglas High School Shooter and think there is definitely something going on here. With McCabe under investigation this incident now shows that this was a pattern of corruption coming out the FBI Building, and also a larger pattern of incompetence.

At this time, what are we the American people supposed to think? We know both James Comey and Andrew McCabe both

JAMES COMEY

ABSOLUTELY NO LOYALTY

By: Elliott Lew Griffin

tell lies, and I'm pretty sure they have both been doing so for a very very long time. And I mean they have both done a whole host of other things and they haven't gone to jail yet? But the real question is? Are they going to even try to lock them up? We see that Comey just got a multi-million-dollar book deal and have gotten paid to do a lot of interviews. And to me, the entire time Comey has continued to tell this false narrative of how he mistakenly meddled in our election, but we all know this is not true. His inaccurate account of what really happened aren't adding up. If anything, they're adding up to the fact that he's an obitual liar, point blank simple.

Now I would buy the book to try to figure out where he's lying and what more evidence he's consciously revealing, but I'm not spending my money and or time to support his crap. Then besides what does that matter anyway, we know that he's lied on multiple occasions. We know that he's meddled in our 2016 Presidential election at a rate twice as much as any Russian ever could, along with a whole host of other crimes and he still allowed to parade around our country and sell books on his book tour. Like I say this really behooves me period. To me, if he was allowed to parade around our country it should have been in shackles, along with two officers escorting him to his cell. And I'm sorry, but the headline should have read... "We got that ******* that meddled in our 2016 presidential election". Like I say, this is how it should have went folk.

We have spent hours and hours talking about Russia meddling in our election, but even though we have found that to be true and are not true, no Russians will ever be held accountable for

JAMES COMEY

ABSOLUTELY NO LOYALTY

By: Elliott Lew Griffin

their actions do to non-extradition policies we have with Russia . However, we have James Comey who Trump calls slippery James Comey and I personally believe that has some truth to it because Comey has been able to commit all of these federal crimes against us in our country and has been able to slip by without prosecution every time. By Comey abusing his power to interfere with our presidential election this is a serious crime against our democracy. We let him do it today and guess what somebody's going to do it again to us tomorrow. We should not take this lightly folks. I will say Trump has come down pretty hard on Russia more and more as time has gone on. He is even working with them more and more as time has gone on especially with Syria , but to me the heck was spending money investigating Russian meddling in our 2016 election, we have to spend our resources investigating James Comey who accomplished that and more. Or how about investigating the women's cases that we talked about in mass incarceration piece of America. And or conducting a thorough investigation as to where are the kids that trump took under their freaking zero tolerance policy that they haven't returned. I mean seriously, can we get our kids back, and or do we have a 100% tolerance for that. And Like I say it must be 99.9% because I'm definitely not on board with that one. And hey you got to exclude yourself.... Like I always tell people, this is not a game or a drill neither folks. And it sure in the heck isn't practice folks. So, to Trump and Congress CAN WE GET BACK OUR KIDS ARE WHAT??? Can you at least convene a hearing so that we could question the people that were last known to have the missing kids? I mean can we get anything out of these people folks? AND THAT'S WHY

JAMES COMEY

ABSOLUTELY NO LOYALTY

By: Elliott Lew Griffin

I HATE THESE PEOPLE AND YOU SHOULD TOO BECAUSE THEIR IMBECELES I KEEP TELLING YOU!!!

You know what, yeah sure James Comey should be going to jail folks, but please don't act like you guys didn't sit up here and listen to this guy lie to you for days on end already. Had it been me he would have been gone. "Sir- Did you take the documents from the FBI Building and give them to your friend. (OKAY- IT'S OVER FOLKS. THAT'S THEFT FROM THE FBI BUILDING AND UNCLE SAM. THAT'S TREASON AGAINST THE AMERICAN PEOPLE. THAT'S LEAKING GOVERMENTAL INFORMATION.... AND HAVE LIED TO GOD.... CONGRESS AND EVERYBODY ELSE IN BETWEEN....

THEN THEY SAY WELL HOW DID HE LIE TO GOD...WELL HE TOOK AN OATH UNDER GOD TO UPHOLD THE CONSTITUTION AND THE PEOPLE RIGHT?

THEN LIKE I SAY HAD HE HAD THIS INFORMATION OR WHATEVER HE THOUGHT IT WAS OR COULD BE (which we all know now was nothing anyway right) HE SHOULD OF STOOD UP GUT SUCKED IN – CHEST POKED OUT AND BLEW THE WHISTLE.... But no, he didn't. Sorry! YEAH SORRY ABOUT HIS LUCK, BUT HE CREATED IT RIGHT AND THEREFORE SHOULD BE JAILED FOR IT RIGHT...LAW AND ORDER RIGHT...LAW AND ORDER RIGHT??? Yeah right, we'll see (and please don't forget real patriots are watching...real patriots are watching.)

Naw, I swear these people be thinking like people left home already...no folks we're right here watching them screw us again, royally. Wake up folks, wake up folks because that's all I have to say is just wake up period.

I mean how could we never have prosecuted Comey already. And this has gone on forever and ever and ever already. I doubt if it's going to stop by the time, he testifies on September 30th, 2020.

OMG, maybe this book would have reached there before he reaches his end conclusion of lies that he's told you guys again and again, or hey maybe you could take it for what it is this time and figure out what he's lying about and or if you're going to prosecute him or you just goanna talk to him or you just want him in the news cycle again this close to election time and or probably all thee above and more. And again, I could probably guess it's not to hand cuff him, lock him up and prosecute him then.

And too boot folks, all of this money, resources, time, effort and energy we spent on all of this, has been in vein if we don't get James Comey. All I can say is he knew about everything, even including the Russian Steele Dossier. Why? Because again, even if we found the Russia hackers are the trollers they aren't going to jail. This whole time has been nothing but a waste of time. Nobody's going to jail folks, not even James Comey. And that's why I say, to me that was a waste of time and no money oh and more money trying to prosecute someone that we more likely will never see period now with Russia and trump collusion investigation still ongoing and Bob Mueller will eventually arrive at that conclusion on that of course we concluded that and we found that to be not true. Again sorry, most of this book was

JAMES COMEY

ABSOLUTELY NO LOYALTY

By: Elliott Lew Griffin

written whenever James Comey published his book, so hey I'm just trying to correct some of the facts to get you up to speed on how long we have been onto to this dude Comey for real folks. You can't make this stuff up. This dude then really did all of this and more in this book. I mean come on James Comey was also one of the main reasons we wanted to hire the Special Counsel Robert Mueller to come in and investigate all of this. It was only later that I found out that Robert Mueller was Comey's friend. They were buddies, pows, and remarkably close friends. And hey let's not forget out of all of this Bob Mueller concluded his conclusions and, in his conclusions, there was no collusions of any kind by the Trump administration. There was nothing, not even a modicum of evidence to support any of it...the Russian Hoax folks. Like, you know you heard Mueller conclude there was nothing folks. And like I say, You would think the Demoncrats would come out and at least say I'm sorry for disrespecting the country and taking us through that you know what I'm saying, but again of course, nothing.

As a person that likes to stick to the real facts and those facts reveal that James Comey meddled in our 2016 election and committed several punishable...I mean rehabilitable. Again, Capitol Hill is goanna have a chance to question him again on September 30th and like I say, what are they going to do folks. The explanations he's given so far about doing so and so and such and such, in all of his interviews are so far from the truth that the whole world knows this dude is lying. And if they buy this again of September 30th, they got to be done folks. Like I say, if they don't prosecute him, then the message is clear we got to vote them folks out. Why? Because obviously they enjoy

84

JAMES COMEY

ABSOLUTELY NO LOYALTY

By: Elliott Lew Griffin

watching chaos and confusion and doing nothing about it. It's like Trump said, these people support lawlessness. And then that's why I'm back to I don't care what Comey says he's violated several FBI rules when he acted. That to me shows his criminal intent period. Now if he didn't violate almost every longstanding FBI policy, then I would say maybe, just maybe it was a mistake, but the fact that he violated so many ethic and judicial FBI rules in doing so, to me clearly put Slippery Shady James Comey on the hook for all these (real) (not so called felonies) that Comey has committed against U.S., including the fact that he should be on the hook for corruptly meddling in our 2016 Presidential election. So again, hopefully Congress is going to do their job and or something about it when they have him on Capitol Hill on September 30th, 2020. The world is watching...please let us know.

I tell you what, the more and more Comey opens his mouth the more and more less credible he gets. Then when I look at the title of his book again, we're back to the fact that he can't even tell the truth about that. Like seriously, when is this dude ever going to tell the truth. And how can you just wake up one day and start telling so many lies now? Life just doesn't work that way I'm sorry.

I'm telling you; this is that governmental double standard crapola that we been talking about. Again, corruption at its finest and Congress is corrupt if they turn a blind eye to it again. Then like I say this is too much to turn a blind eye too. Here, Comey committed several crimes and should be punished (excuse me rehabilitated for committing those crimes).

JAMES COMEY

ABSOLUTELY NO LOYALTY

By: Elliott Lew Griffin

It's kind of like the Trump Russia hotel story, where Comey doesn't have no evidence to back it up. "So why put that in your book then?" And this is the information in his book, not mine. He said these crapola stories to try to sell a book, not me. I'm just here reporting on James Comey and I'm pretty sure there are other ways to sell a book then to right a fabricated and elaborate story like that. I mean why would you even put that in there. We're talking about the president United States and he's the freaking head director of the FBI. So again, why would you even put that in there that doesn't even make sense. No of course, it's just more lies on lies. Then of course now he's writing his new book called "Saving Justice" but yet on the other hand we know James Comey has "Murdered Justice". So if James Comey does put out his book "Saving Justice", then please be on the lookout for the real truth... "James Comey Murdered Justice" See Comey, Truth has already got it's boots on and there waiting for you.

That's why the quote by Virginia Woolf stands out to me where she says: "If you do not tell the truth about yourself you cannot tell it about other people". Here slippery Shady James Comey can't even tell the truth about himself let alone anyone else. And that's why I say I think that quote goes a long way with what we're talking about Here today. That if you're not trustworthy in one area (YOURSELF) then you can't be trustworthy in another or at least you can but hey eventually you're going to be untrustworthy that's the whole conclusion to that statement. And that's why I don't believe nothing James Comey says because he lacks credibility period. Now if he had came out and said you know what America I'm sorry and

JAMES COMEY

ABSOLUTELY NO LOYALTY

By: Elliott Lew Griffin

admitted guilt then I would say he has gained insight into the crimes that even committed.

But the fact that he keeps claiming it was all just a big mistake when he corruptly violated FBI protocol, I'm not buying it and you shouldn't either. For real I'm not buying it and it would be a shame to let this crook slip by with his lame excuses of why he did it. I mean he could continue to come here and use his FBI tactics to play Congress and or people against each other all he wants. But for crying out loud arrest that man in the process.

The crazy part is, I even seen Comey on late night talk shows like it's funny, The only problem is James Comey really assaulted our democracy and should never be able to sit up here and laugh about it on T.V. Maybe with some Russians, and or his cellmate, but definitely not against America on late night T.V. Why, because his laughing sure wasn't with America right? Unless you're against America, right??, and or at least nobody I know laughed about what Comey did. It simply was not funny. And I don't even mean to put the Russians in there you know. I'm quite sure they were tired of hearing about it in their Country too. Like I say, I'm just making it as a statement you know the Russian hoax and everything going on you know what I mean that was proved   to   be   false.

LIKE I SAY HOW ABOUT WE TURN OUR ATTENTION TO FINDING OUR KIDS that freaking was taken in the zero-tolerance policy that would work for us the zero tolerance policy kids back. (OKAY THE ZERO TOLERANCE POLICY KIDS FOLKS. WHY? BECAUSE WE HAVE A ZERO TOLERANCE POLICY OF THEM MISSING...SO PLEASE CAN WE GET CONGRESS ON THAT.)

JAMES COMEY

ABSOLUTELY NO LOYALTY

By: Elliott Lew Griffin

I mean Comey can play the right and the left all he wants, but when you start laughing about cheating us the American people out of our democracy, I'm sorry in no way shape form or fashion is it funny. Then that's like a crime of mental in our election. i.e. crime of passion because now he's urking my brain and that's not good. Forreal, like who just does that and laughs on late night T.V. about it. And to me this was the most serious crime he committed on our country, but since he's committed sooo many crimes that he should be convicted and imprisoned for them. So, my only question is where is justice? I know Comey has lied to Congress on more than one occasion. I mean what did he say he didn't know that the guy he gave those memos too was going to leak them to the press? I don't really care whether he knew the guy was going to leak them or not, that's all irrelevant because Comey knew that just by taking them from the FBI building and giving them to his associate was leaking them. Once he took them from the FBI Building that was a theft. Then once he gave them to someone, right then and there that was a leak. If they made it to the press, it doesn't matter because he wasn't supposed to show or give them to anybody. Again, he wasn't supposed to take them from the building. So again, when he's taking them from the building right and giving them to his friend right, he's leaking information, come on folks get real. This is not a game, get real folks. So, when they convene the Senate on September 30th, they should lock him up right then and there. Have heart, have money. He shouldn't be able to pass go and sure in the heck shouldn't be able to collect $200 dollars.

Then his whole narrative of a higher loyalty is blown out of proportion because if he saying he gave those memos to his

JAMES COMEY

ABSOLUTELY NO LOYALTY

By: Elliott Lew Griffin

associate for a higher loyalty, then he knew they were going to be leaked to the press? That to me further defies the logic of a higher loyalty when he claims he didn't know that they were going to be leaked to the press. That's why I'm saying nothing he says is adding up even a little bit. Is any of that making sense? Like I say "NO". Nothing he says is making sense folks.

I don't know, but I will tell you this, if we allow Slippery Shady James Comey to slip by without hiring a second special counsel to investigate him, then we might as well throw in the towel because that just means in America we have no accountability for those at the top period. "NO" at the bottom due to overcharging, but at the top we have almost no charging and or selective charging we should call it right? Our government selective charging folks. And, actually really vulnerable to corruption and coveruption. (They should even add that word to the English dictionary "coveruption" Is when you cover up corruption). Like my mom says my grandpa used to say all the time growing up as a kid...thank me thank me.

But like I say, this is corruption and coveruption at its finest and the world is watching. And just look, James Comey is laughing in our face at cashing in on us at the bank, even after he committed all those crimes against our nation. Like they say, Comey committed not just one, not just two, but Comey committed a few crimes and to me it was a few too many to allow him to slip away with it.

How can you beyond a reasonable doubt violate FBI protocol and say it was a mistake? To me, which one was the mistake, the violation of FBI protocol or the meddling in the 2016 presidential election. They both were crimes. That's why I say everything he says is a lie. I started off writing this book kind of as a joke about James Comey having absolutely no loyalty, but the more facts that came in about this guy was unbelievable. Like this dude belongs in jail, not getting rich doing a million-dollar book tour.

I'll tell you what folks, all of this just reeks of corruption and coveruption. But hey at this point all I can say is please keep reading...

JAMES COMEY – ABSOLUTELY NO LOYALTY

JAMES COMEY

ABSOLUTELY NO LOYALTY

By: Elliott Lew Griffin

2

CHAPTER 2

JAMES COMEY JUST QUIT LYING OR AT LEAST QUIT TALKING RIGHT

Like they say, PLEAD THE FIFTH, PLEAD THE FIFTH, PLEAD THE FIFTH…. Or worse it's too late, James Comey you're going to jail.

But no like they really say, half-truths are still whole lies, so even if James Comey is telling us half-truths, hashtag they are still whole lies. However, I think he's completely telling us whole lies. I just watched the Jake Tapper CNN interview with Comey and Tapper asks Comey how many trump memos it was, and he answers: He doesn't no, but the whole world knows it's seven. Not to mention the fact that he wrote every single one of them and he supposed to be the only lead witness in that allegation against trump and he doesn't know how many memos he's written and or took? Like yeah, okayyy!

Like this guy is a joke, everything he says is "I don't know or it's possible? Unlikely but possible". He's not giving us much of anything and I believe he owes us a heck of a lot more. He claims he wanted to protect the FBI and its legacy, so why did he not follow the long-standing judicial policies then. He talks about lack of candor, but in his book, he falsely claims that trump was in a Russia hotel room with prostitutes allegedly watching a Golden shower. Hashtag remember that. Then he claimed his book wasn't about trump or he don't hate trump or anything like that, but I don't believe his answers especially anything that has to do with "it's possible". Like what, (shut up stupid!)

He's talked about violating the rule of law, but we know he's done that. He's talked of Andrew McCabe as it's different from him, but the McCabe allegations are the same allegations he's committed. I would say allege cause he's innocent till proven guilty, but we all know what he did?

He talks about having core values for our country, but Meddling in our election is not having core values of the American people, especially where there was alleged to have been an ongoing investigation against both candidates Hillary and trump, yet he only told the public about the Hillary investigation. Again, his answers, not mine. And again, his answers are all incongruent to the facts. I mean can we at least admit that? And that's sad again folks we have Hillary Clinton and Trump and they're both under investigation in 2016, like #WOW. Of course, trump was exonerated of his. The Hillary

JAMES COMEY

ABSOLUTELY NO LOYALTY

By: Elliott Lew Griffin

Clinton investigation still remains large. I think everybody was just happy she didn't try to run for President again in 2020 so they really don't even care anymore. But anyhow....

Comey claims he acted in good faith and he always tries to be transparent. Like OK, and which one of his answers am I supposed to believe on that one? I swear, the only thing that's saving Comey right now from a full assault on his character, integrity and candor is, both sides are using part of what he's saying to fit their narrative, and or viewpoints and is still hard to do. Why, because both sides have said at one point or another that they don't believe many of his answers.

My thing is, when does not believing his answers, turn into Comey's just flat out lying. Then, how can we take him seriously? Where are we to separate his story from facts to fiction. If we don't know what to believe then again, to me, it's all a lie. I mean this was the head guy at the FBI and he writes a book talking about trumps' hand-size and I dare not ask what guy writes about a guys hand size and an obvious fake news story about a Golden shower in attempt to sell books

I'll tell you what? If the Trump's Golden shower rumors true, how does Comey know about it? Was he there? Did he go see one afterwards and they told him Trump was just here? Do you see what I mean??? All a lie.... Then Comey further claims That trump runs his life like a mob boss and everyone around him as loyal, then he definitely didn't hear it from no one in the Trump Organization, so (listen) the only way Comey could have gotten that allege information was for my question? And my question is which Russian did he get it from? The Russian he threw our

JAMES COMEY

ABSOLUTELY NO LOYALTY

By: Elliott Lew Griffin

2016 Presidential Election for? Or did he make it all up? Again, we're talking about James Comey here- absolutely he's lying.

Up until this point we have heard a year worth of rhetoric of how the Russians meddled in our elections and we know James Comey threw our election at the end. So maybe Congress could put two and two together because it definitely equals 4 every day of the week. Hey, we can even use a Comey answer on this one "it's possible". I mean how can he say that about trump and get away with it. Then he uses "it's not true" or "it could have been" or "it's possible" or "he doesn't know" but isn't that still some kind of slander. Putting out facts and rumors that's not true. Isn't that where the 1st Amendment says wait a stinking minute. Remember freedom of speech only goes so far before you turn into the twerp for those words. And not saying it didn't happen, but I'm saying if you have no proof that it happened, or that it didn't happen, then hey what do you have again folks you have nothing Idol pages on Comey's book talking about nothing. Again, lies on lies. And Trump's hand size. Like I say, let's see what happens on September 30th. How many questions he actually knows and how many times he says he doesn't know or that it's possible or at least I hope he says let me check my notes this time.

Honestly, I don't know what to believe, I know I can't believe James Comey, so I have to start going with something logical. Everyone in their right mind should know that James Comey is a pathological liar by now. He sits less than 30 minutes in a Jake Tapper interview and everyone who watched it at some point, or another can honestly say some of his answers was really

JAMES COMEY

ABSOLUTELY NO LOYALTY

By: Elliott Lew Griffin

unbelievable? That's why I said when...When does it go from Comey's answers were just unbelievable? To you know what? Comey is a pathological liar.

Even at times when Comey wasn't telling his lies...hashtag his half-truths still equated to whole lies. To be honest, for that reason I'm sad to see that James Comey's book sold so well. To me, that's the same thing as if we were paying him to sell us out. I believe that not only hurt our democracy, but shattered our sense of accountability, credibility honesty, integrity, and every other word you could probably find imaginable. Our sense of decency and everything else in between that fits in that realm of synonyms and homonyms and tailored to fit the fixture of that metaphor.

To date, we have allowed Slippery Shady James Comey to get away unshackled, unrestrained, and unrehabilitated, so now it comes as no surprise to see that next head guy in the FBI Andrew McCabe do exactly the same thing.

We all just witnessed the Department of Justice issue an explosive report on McCabe where he leaked and misled investigators over the Clinton investigated for his own personal gain, but didn't Comey do the exact same thing? That's what happens when there is no accountability, you get rid of 1 and the saga continues.

I'll tell you what, since the Justice Department just submitted a criminal referral on Andrew McCabe and we now have Comey saying he could well be a witness against McCabe, we should play them against each other. Tell McCabe that if he tells on

JAMES COMEY

ABSOLUTELY NO LOYALTY

By: Elliott Lew Griffin

Comey, we will give him the best deal ever. It's called Nothing because he's going to jail too. We seriously got to stop giving people who tell on people deals when they were 100% in on it when they were doing it, right? I am so sorry, but snitches are people who tell or whatever the case may but remember 9 times or ten times out of ten it's only when they get caught. However, when they get caught, we should give them the same amount of time. Why? Because they were 100% in on it when they were doing it, right? Now they're only 50% in on it or 20% in on it or however much less time or leniency they get to get out of it. It's like after they get caught {Snitch Nine} for example, he tells and he's out of jail, and or only getting 10% of the time. So that means he was only 10% in on the crime? No, I'm sorry he was 100% in on the crime and he should be doing 100% of the time like his cohort or wherever they are, right?

In any event like they say, they know it's the FBI way, he tells on the bigger fish and he'll get a good deal. In this case, Comey is the bigger fish. It's the same thing Mueller and the FBI been doing to Michael Flynn, Paul Manafort and now Michael Cohen, hoping they roll over on trump. However, we have a key now and that is Comey has already said he's willing to testify on Andrew McCabe, so we'll tell McCabe look would Comey just said, and he better tell on him first period.

Hey this is the real live FBI way. It's been going on forever folks, so please don't act like you don't know. And like they say, don't let Comey tell on you McCabe, tell on him first. Then hey McCabe might even get Trump to pardon him, you saw Scooter Libby and Paul Manafort get a pardon, so I don't see why he wouldn't get one, especially since you know he told on Trumps arch nemesis (who wrongfully tried to get him indicted) Comey.

However, in any event like I say, James Comey the one that got the whole trump Russia hoax collusion investigation going to begin with folks. You heard Comey in his Jake Tapper interview that he leaked his memos. However, you missed what he said: he leaked his memos. The head guy at the FBI leaked his memos. Like I always say what else did he leak folks, come on now let's not be naive here. And by the way isn't that treason.

Like that's wicked? Trump fired him and he made up some crap on one of his memos alleging trump tried to obstruct him and he leaked them to his friends with hopes to get Trump, the President of the United States impeached and unseated. (And it was all a hoax folks) Yeah, that sounds like treason (Comey abusing his FBI powers to try to get the sitting President of our Country indicted), yeah okayyyy??? Like I say Comey should be imprisoned for it...All of it

So now we know Comey got a lot of this going and he's been away to get away with all of this Scott free. And why did he make all of this up. I guess the question and or the answer is simple, he only made them up after Trump fired him. Remember Comey threw the 2016 Presidential Election for someone and he may very well have done it to help the Republican Party win. Remember James Comey (Republican) But then what I believe happened was Comey was looking for some kind of recognition from Trump for throwing the election against Hillary at the end. Trump of course is Trump and of course Trump won on his own. He didn't even take into account that Comey threw the election for him and the Republican party at the end. And after that Comey got bitter, then sour when Trump fired him. Now folks he made it all up. It's called the disgruntled ex-employee, right? We've all heard about it, but now James Comey did more than just be a disgruntled ex-employee, he took it several steps forward by committing a boat load of crimes and the sad part is it was all a hoax folks. The James Comey hoax folks....

That's why I don't believe a word of what the memo says. Again, if he had evidence like that he should have immediately went to the DOJ, and he didn't. The question is why, and the answer is simple and again I told you it's because trump fired him. James Comey was a disgruntled ex-employee who thought his employer owed him something for so called helping him get elected. I'm telling you, we're not to far off. And Congress knows, I'm just wondering if they are going to continue to do selective prosecution or prosecute James Comey this time, or what?

We don't believe nothing Comey says and I can't even believe he admitted to leaking in the Tapper CNN interview. For that his credibility is forever ruined because it clearly shows a vendetta since he only leaked after he was fired. But again, he only leaked his not true memos after he was fired. So yes, this hoax was Perpetrated by none other than James Comey himself. Our head guy at the FBI. Then after that the number two guy Andrew McCabe goes rogue. Like I we got to look for the number three guy in charge now.... What's his name Christopher Wray. Yeah, we got to keep a crystal ray on him ok, Okay!

Then they're payed Comey multi-millions of dollars for a book deal and countless interviews where we still don't believe many

JAMES COMEY

ABSOLUTELY NO LOYALTY

By: Elliott Lew Griffin

of us answers and for that our American sense of normalcy is going out the window. He's even writing a new book again like I told you it's called James Comey Saving Justice. But we just talked about the Russian hoax that he perpetuated with his stolen in leaked memos that he himself written. After that if we let him walk out the Congress building on September 30th, we stand to morally disvalue our country in front of the world with this type of disrespectful behavior. Lies on top of lies on top of lies. It seems to be all that we hear from our politicians and those that we have put in charge. Again, where does this stop. We see a breakdown from the FBI all the way down to the police. From the police all the way up to the top director of the FBI building. And they're supposed to be stopping the criminals and I'm sorry to say are the criminals themselves. How do you stop the criminals and are the criminals that's both hypocrisy and an assault on our democracy?

James Comey meddled in our 2016 presidential election and leaked memos that he more likely than not didn't write until he was fired that's why he didn't produce them until after he was fired and were paying him. (Man) the Slippery Slope James Comey strikes again and striking with another book Saving Justice. But don't worry folks, we're ahead of the game this time. We're not going to wait for the lies to get all the way around the world and back around before the truth got it's boots on. This time we'll be right there waiting on him. If he's writing James Comey Saving Justice; then folks guess what we're writing James Comey Murdered Justice. Why? Because again James Comey Murdered Justice. (All Rights reserved on the book Title)

By: Elliott Lew Griffin

And again, can't you see how he's lying to you. Oh, James Comey Saving Justice! What a crock. All a lie. And where does it stop from there. "I don't know I can't recall". I mean at least act like a real FBI Director and be like, hey let me check my notes. I mean I'm pretty sure he has some notes somewhere right. I mean are we going to demand that proof or we're going to let him get away with "I don't know I can't recall" more lies.

I mean even when you look at the Jake Tapper interview where it made me walk away like, I didn't believe some of his answers and it was on questions that really had no relevance, so if he would not be completely truthful in giving those answers, then what makes me think he's going to be truthful in any other answer at all.... And again, James Comey strikes again. He'll be back at the Senate on September 30th for what round 3 or is this 4. To be honest I can't even remember anymore, but hey the circus parlay continues. And hey I guess this story is getting more interested by the second. All I can say is stay tuned folks, you're reading...

JAMES COMEY – ABSOLUTELY NO LOYALTY

COMEY
WE'RE COMING
FOR YOU

CHAPTER 3

JAMES COMEY
A HABITUAL LIAR

I'm going to start off this chapter by saying how many times must we accept I don't know answers from James Comey before we conclude he's a habitual liar? Seriously?? I don't know, I already discovered it and now I'm just here to try to help you find inner peace with it. They always say, if you tell one line, you got to keep telling more and more to keep it covered up. One thing about the truth, it adds up and I'm pretty sure we can all see at some point or another that what Comey is telling us is not adding up, so it shouldn't come as no surprise to keep hearing him lie, lie, lie to keep it covered up. That's where they get the term once a liar, always a liar from cause once you tell one lie you got to keep telling lies on top of lies to keep it cover up. That's why Michael E MONTAIGNE quote fits perfectly here because it says: "Unless a man feels he has a good enough memory, he should never venture to lie." I guess somebody should have told James Comey that because I have come to realize that he doesn't have a good enough memory to keep all his lies straight. Like William Paley have said: "White lies introduce others of a darker complexion" and I'm here to report to you folks that Comey's white lies have gone pitch black today. It's gotten so dark that it won't even work to try to cut on the lights anymore folks, flood lights won't even work for Comey right now.

How come he has been able to avoid prosecution so far, I don't know? Your guess is just as good as mine. All I can do is quote Donald Trump and say he's Slippery folks.

I'll tell you what? The best lie I heard Comey tell so far is he did all of his alleged corruption for us folks. It was all for higher loyalty to us the American people. Or at least that's what his book is alluding too. I would say if his intentions were for the overall good of the American people, I would hate to see what his bad intentions look like. I swear, if me and you did what he did, and said we did it for the good of the American people, we could forget being in jail, we would be buried underneath it. I guess that's why they call him Slippery Shady James Comey because he's the only slimeball that's able to get away with it all.

To me, and I'm pretty sure to many other people, Comey has lost all sense of reality by the many lies and half-truths he told to date, that there is not a snowball chance in hell that we should be congratulated him or paying him for all the crimes that he'd bestowed upon us in our country. I know everybody wants to hear about what James Comey had to say about Donald Trump, but we heard it from the people that read it already, that there's nothing new in there under the sun. Maybe a few more lies, coupled with a few more half-truths and "I don't know", "I can't recall", "I don't remember", and or the many "it's possible" statements he's made.

I mean seriously, how much could he personally know about Donald Trump, trump fired him on May 9th, 2017, just a little over 100 days into his presidency? Of course it comes as no surprise that Comey would have nothing to talk about trump, but his hand or his shoe size, or whatever else he talked about, his eye tanning lines because let's face it folks, he has nothing else salacious to talk about. Other than again, a fabricated golden shower folks because we can't forget that one either. #WOW

What else did he say, Donald Trump runs his family and his presidency like a mob boss? The crazy part is I think someone from the FBI had said something similar like that about Hillary and how she runs her Clinton organization like a crime family. I don't really know about Comey, Trump or Hillary, but everybody I know would prefer to have truthful, honest and loyal people around them, so for Comey to try to cite that as a moral defect, and or a character defect against Trump, only shows us another example of his immoral defects in his own character. He can't find honest, trustworthy and loyal people to be around him. That's probably because Comey does lying, sneaky, corrupt weasel moves all the time.

Who wouldn't want loyal people around them folks, everybody but James Comey, right? I run my family like a Mob Boss because I expect them to be honest, trustworthy and loyal...yeah Comey okayyy. Like they say when you lie in bed with Wolves, you wake up with fleas. Like they say, what is

105

JAMES COMEY

ABSOLUTELY NO LOYALTY

By: Elliott Lew Griffin

loyalty other than expecting a person to be faithful? I guess we now know that faithful is nowhere in James Comey. It's so bad that I'm pretty sure James Comey can't even be loyal to himself. Every interview he just keeps downplaying his story until it's just now, "I don't know folks". He probably doesn't believe that there is a thing called loyalty in the world and it shows because he's definitely didn't have no loyalty to us the American people. Or the oath that he took, remember that.

I'll tell you what I just found out and it's getting worser by the second. What can I say folks, the Comey story has gone from bad to worse? The long waited for Comey memos was just released yesterday. In a March 30th, 2017 memo that Comey wrote about a summarized phone call between him and trump, Comey wrote that trump told him to keep looking into the corruption of the people and get this "satellites" around him. Therefore, that memo report alone shows that trump was not trying to obstruct justice or shut down the collusion investigation that Comey has claimed for a year now. Sorry to report to everyone that was hoping for an obstruction of justice charge on Trump, Comey lied to you. What can I say, it's all fake news folks?

And there is a lot more, and I'm going to save some more of the Comey memo details for the next chapter. I can't give it to you all at once, to say the least it's a lot to take in. (And if I did, I wouldn't have a book, right?) But if you haven't heard about it, then you might want to be sitting down when I tell it to you. Like I always say, if you heard it before, don't worry, you haven't heard it like I'm going to tell it to you, that's for sure.

JAMES COMEY

ABSOLUTELY NO LOYALTY

By: Elliott Lew Griffin

At this point I guess I will give you a quote by Tyron Edwards and it says: "Hell is truth seen too late", and I say that because James Comey is hell seen too late. I don't know about you, but every time I see him, I think what the hell is he's lying to us about this time. Like again, tell the truth and shame the devil sometimes Comey.

I'm sorry I know all of this appears fictional, but I'm going to tell you right now, that I'm not that good of a storyteller to make all this stuff up folks. I wish I were, but I'm not. Do I dare go back to the fact that James Comey titled his book a higher loyalty, but then in that same book he criticized trump for expecting the people around him to have a higher loyalty. How odd is that huh? Now your starting to get the point huh. Like #WOW how true is that. And I guess that's why Comey's not around him anymore. He didn't have a higher loyalty. Or worse, Absolutely No Loyalty. To be fair, I don't think James Comey has a higher loyalty bone in his body. Or does he even have a loyalty bone in his body. A lower loyalty bone, any kind of bone. Well folks I guess he got a backbone cause he's still sitting up there telling you lies and you're still going for it. And he still sitting up there telling you lies and you're going for it. And he's still free, so I guess he's laughing on late night T.V. about them, not perse you or me.

I'll tell you what, if Comey was ever going for a higher loyalty to the American people, then I'm glad he wasn't asked as the FBI director to ever do an honorable 21 gun salute because he definitely don't know which way is up, and or how to shoot. Why? Because every time he lies, I swear he's shooting himself in the foot. They say aim for the stars and you'll at least hit the moon, but with Comey's higher loyalty strategy I would say he never even aimed for the mountains, cause his aim for a higher loyalty to us the American people, never made it off the ground.

I was watching the news the other day and they asked in the case of Comey versus Trump who do you believe? I'll tell you what? If you can't believe Comey then it doesn't matter, there is no case to be heard. And right now, Comey claims of events with the president is going down in flames, they even said that Comey's memos will be attached as exhibit A for Trump's obstruction of justice defense.

At this point, what more can I say we're talking about James Comey here and everybody knows we're talking about James Comey here? Didn't know, now you know. I'll tell you what folks, there might be a lot more you didn't know, so if you want to know more please don't fret and keep reading...Your Reading....

JAMES COMEY – ABSOLUTELY NO LOYALTY

3

CHAPTER 4

JAMES COMEY
A SERIAL LEAKER

What more can I say folks, you're reading about James Comey absolutely no loyalty. This is not a game, James Comey is a real leaker, but if I were you, I would worry because his lie is, he did it for us the American people. You know what comes to mind when I think about James Comey's leaking, is the Clorox bleach commercial where the kid in the bathrooms trying to get his belt undone and when he can't get it done he calls out…. "mom we have a situation".

Well I tell you what folks, if we were to do a grown-up version of that commercial, the grown-up kid will be none other than James Comey because he definitely can't hold his water. They say bleach may have helped Hillary out of her email situation, but it's definitely not going to help Comey. I know from experience that when bleach can't clean up a situation, it's over. What can I say, both Comey and Hillary is personally stained forever?

Yeah, you might think I'm playing, but I'm telling you what they're saying, don't share with Comey confidential secrets, he's going to leak them. He can't help himself. He got pee pee stains on his hands. Like they say don't even dare ask Comey if he was the one that leaked it, you already know he's going to lie to you and say, "No McCabe did it". Or in this case, he might even say he did it and still don't go to jail, where they do that at. The crazy part is in James Comey's Clorox bleach commercial his mom will walk in on him standing in a puddle of pee and she asked him son did you pee pee on yourself and he'll answer no mom- Trump's Russian Golden shower girls did it. The mom asks the son- we'll where did they go? Comey would look around and still lie while pointing and stating out the window. Or worse, "I don't know".

For real, I'm sorry, only made that story up to show you how weird Comey was for even putting that in his book. Seriously Comey talks of having higher values and morals, but he puts a story like that in there that more likely than not is all false. I mean seriously, all his lies, coupled with examples like that in this book and I can't take nothing he says seriously. I know I just did it, but I did it to correct the facts and as a prime example to show how weird he was for doing it in the 1st place. Come on that's the real kind of lying FBI Serial Leaker Slippery Shady James Comey is. The crazy part is leading up to the

JAMES COMEY

ABSOLUTELY NO LOYALTY

By: Elliott Lew Griffin

2016 presidential election there was a stream of leaks coming out of FBI. Again, more likely than not Comey.

On October 26, 2016 Rudy Giuliani which just so happens to be Trump's new attorney went on Fox news and promised a surprise or two that you were going to hear about it next two days. Not surprising two days later James Comey right on cue sent this letter to Congress reopening the Hillary Clinton email investigation. Like . they say who else could have known that Comey was going to send a letter to Congress reopening the Hillary Clinton email investigation, I believe it was Comey himself? Unless he wants to blame it on McCabe now.

Anyhow there's more, on November 4th, 2016, Rudy Giuliani went back on Fox news and confirmed that he had advance warning from a source. Rudy said an interview did he hear about it? "You darn right I heard about it" Giuliani said.

Then, several months later senator Pat Leahy of Vermont in the Senate Judiciary Committee questioned Comey about whether anybody in the FBI during the 2016 campaign have any contact with Rudy Giuliani about the Clinton investigation? Here, the clincher to that story was when Comey said, "it was a matter the FBI is looking into and that he was extremely interested to learn the truth". Comey goes on stating "I don't know yet, but if I find out the people were leaking information about our investigations whether to reporters or private parties, there will be severe consequences".

JAMES COMEY

ABSOLUTELY NO LOYALTY

By: Elliott Lew Griffin

The crazy part is folks, Comey may very well have been the serial leaker the entire time. If he did it once, or twice, what is there to stop me from thinking he did it 3 or 4 or 5000 times. He probably was leaking information about all of his federal investigations. To think, Comey had everybody in the FBI Building running around looking for the leaker. Comey vowing there will be severe consequences for the leaker once he was caught and lo and behold it was Comey his crying partner McCabe, the two guys at the top leaking all of our classified information. Ha-ha! The last two people everyone would suspect. Was again, lo and behold, the suspects.

#WOW. However, I just want to know the truth period since really Rudy Giuliani is now working for Trump as his attorney, I want to know will he tell us who his source was and if it was Comey, then bam, he's really going to jail for lying to Congress folks? Said he had no communication with Giuliana, but Giuliani knows? That's probably why Trump went and hired him to put it into the Mueller probe because he got a secret source against none other than AKA Slippery Shady James Comey.

I'll tell you with all this talk about Comey testifying on McCabe, I wouldn't be at all surprised to hear that McCabe flipped and ready to roar as a prosecution witness against Comey. It's all getting distrusting folks especially with James Comey testifying again on September 30th, 2020 in front of Congress. It's getting so serious that I might have to slow down and get a little more serious. I say that because people tend to laugh at what I have to say even though they know that I'm serious. But I'll tell you serious folks, don't laugh today because there is a lot of information that Comey is revealing in his book tour interviews that is going to become useful in the upcoming investigation against him. And don't worry I have it all right here for you folks.

No, I want it to be known that I'm in no way shape or form taking sides in this book. I know we got the left on one side and the right on the other and from what I know both sides have been brutally scorned by James Comey. Someone said that makes him a partial are bipartisan. I Honestly don't think so. The unrefuted evidence shows that he was initially on the right side and then after Trump on the right fired him, he decided to try to go back to the left with a kind of promise to tell on Trump, but again he didn't have nothing to say because he was fired within like 100 days. However, it never happened and worse the story on Comey was getting more damaging. However, I was still shocked to see how the people on the left just opened their arms to Comey after what he did to #Hillary Clinton.

Here's why I said the first part of that last statement is because 11 days to the election, Comey comes out and makes the announcement that the Hillary Clinton investigation is reopened again, but at the same time he didn't announce that the Trump campaign had an ongoing investigation as well. According to Comey's twisted UN logical testimony he gave in his book tour interview, he contends that he told the public about the Hillary investigation because he felt they had a right to know, but I'm assuming from his perspective that the public didn't have a right to know about the alleged Trump investigation? Maybe at the time he knew it was all based on a fake Russian dossier, right? Hey, taking the play book from Comey "it's possible". I mean look we look at the Russian dossier and then we look at Brianna Taylor and what do we find…. We find that we have prosecutors going to the judges and lying about inaccurate information and getting FISA warrants, a freaking home invasion warrants to go in there and kill people. Fake dossier, fake FISA warrants, fake search warrants, fake news, fake people, fake politicians, wow where are we at folk's, Fake lies Matter, Fake lies matter.

But then of course Comey goes on to say more. He claims that at the time he didn't know much about the trump investigation, but in that case he reopened the Hillary email investigation two days before he got the warrant to read the new suspected emails, (did you get that), so technically he didn't know much about the Hillary investigation at that time either, therefore, we must assume he's lying about that too.

Nothing Comey has said to date has made any sense of why he interfered with our 2016 presidential election. And I'm going to tell you why? Because he can't give us an honest answer, that's why?? Therefore, we must assume that it was for a corrupt one. Like I say Trump won, he's our President, and none of this was written to delegitimize him, but in this case, we just want Comey jailed for meddling in our Democratic election.

The crazy part is, it shouldn't even matter which side you're on because at the end of the day, both sides should be against James Comey and what he did to our Country. I'll be honest and tell you right now, I'm 100% partisan against James Comey. Come on Comey just wrote a horrible book about Trump just based on the golden shower alone, but in that same token he'll tell us in his Tapper CNN interview that he doesn't even dislike President Trump. I can't even believe a word he says and at this point if a person wasn't 100% against James Comey, I would just walk away from them because obviously they must like being lied to. And or, there's always the other scenario, they somehow like corruption in their government officials? For that answer I don't know, I'm just throwing that out there as a plausible scenario. Sorry folks!

However, we have new details about the newly released Comey memos and guess what we discovered? That Comey definitely leaked confidential information because not only did Congress redact part of the memos as being classified, but Comey himself had already labeled the bottom of those memos confidential. (Meaning Top Secret Classified Information)

JAMES COMEY

ABSOLUTELY NO LOYALTY

By: Elliott Lew Griffin

So, they say for that reason Slippery Shady James Comey should be going to jail because he violated 18 U. S. C. Section 793 since it's against the law to leak classified information. I don't know, they say it's an open and close case, especially since James Comey classified the memos as classified information (Again meaning confidential) and he already admitted to leaking them to his friends. They say it's going to be like a two minute trial, the prosecutor is going to show the memos to the jury where Comey himself the FBI director and lead investigator in this case, classified the memos as classified and then show his Congress testimony where he admitted to leaking and the jury will have no other option at that point but to find him 100% guilty. I'm sorry James Comey you're going to jail it's just that simple. A 2-minute trial and its over for James Comey. Why? Because he violated 18 U. S. C. Section 793, that's why.

And I'm just reporting the facts as they are coming in and I'll tell you what? If he gets out of this one, then he's really slippery. Man, if that happens, I may quit write books and go to my newfound profession of writing comic books. Make me an animated action figures because move over Marvel there's another comic character in town that Batman, Superman, Iron Man, Robin Hood, Avengers or Black Panther can't catch now.

The Hulk can't grasp him, Spiderman can't web him, and that new comic book character is non other than Slippery Shady James Comey himself folks. At that point,

117

JAMES COMEY

ABSOLUTELY NO LOYALTY

By: Elliott Lew Griffin

James Bond will have nothing on James Comey, the head American FBI Director was better than any James Bond character would ever be. Where is Elliot Ness when you need him? Since Eliot Ness took down the other James...James Capone, I know James Comey can't slip away from him. I know my name is Elliot and James Comey would have been done if it was up to me. So, I guess it's something about those Elliott's' that will catch them every time. And In guess it was Al Capone and not James Capone, but yawl know what I'm talking about. It just sounded good though ha-ha.

Well folks, here goes another startling detail about Comey's memos because there's more. Yeah, a lot more. And this is a good one folks, I guess at a dinner he told one, and sorry let me check my notes to make sure this is correct, I'm sorry it sounds a little crazy to me folks so I just had to triple check what I just reading, so please bear with me folks, we are trying to get this right. James Comey got us all over the place, and he's still out on the streets? Don't worry we're going to lock him up in a minute folks.

OK... I got it, here we go ... Comey's memos that he wrote himself revealed that he told trump... "he's not sneaky , he's not leaky and he don't do weasel moves....", so again do I really got to respond to that folks! I don't even have no come back to that quotation mark that's how bad that is.... All I can say is why did Comey write that folks? I honestly don't know, but I'll also note that Comey said in his Jake Tapper interview that he and I'm

JAMES COMEY

ABSOLUTELY NO LOYALTY

By: Elliott Lew Griffin

paraphrasing it, but that he did his sneaky leaking in attempt to get Trump investigated and get this folks, with these same memos where he wrote he don't do sneaky leaky moves on . All I can say is that James Comey is a weasel folks, that's what you call a weasel move. James Comey – Absolutely No Loyalty.

Well folks, there is a lot more, but if I give it to you all at once I'm pretty sure you'll quit reading and say just convict him already.... I know folks... he's kind of slippery? And kind of Shady...wait we must be talking about none other than James Comey, that weasel. He do weasel moves folks, he do weasel moves. But don't worry folks, we got our best people out there trying to catch him.... Well he's going to the Senate or the Congress on September 30th and hey if they're going to catch him, they got him right their folks. All they have to do is Reach out and grab 'em. Like I said, where is Elliot Ness when you need him? Or better yet where is Elliott, The Make America Amazing guy when you need him right. (Right here tired of listening to James Comey's lies too)

I know the whole world is out there looking for him right now James Comey.... My best guess is he's somewhere doing sneaky leaky weasel moves. (Hey, that is an amazing educated guess) So, if you're looking for James Comey he's probably somewhere doing sneaky leaky weasel moves, so watch out there folks he's kind of tall so you can't miss him, but he's kind of slippery so you might miss him.

Wherever that is, I don't know folks, hopefully it's not somewhere he can get his weasel hands on more top secret confidential classified documents are we might all be in a world of trouble. WikiLeaks all over again. You all know about him, right? They still got him locked up somewhere. And yet Slippery Shady James Comey, the top-secret serial FBI leaker still remains a large. Probably out there leaking our top secrets somewhere and or, probably everywhere. Don't worry folks I don't think he can slip away too much longer, all else fails we're going to call in the Ghostbusters, or maybe even Scooby-Doo. What more can I say folks, but please keep reading...

JAMES COMEY – ABSOLUTELY NO SECRETS

Oh, oh, I'm sorry folks, wait a minute, that was my contemporaneous notes for the sequel. It might be coming out soon. Until then sorry about the interruption you're reading ...

JAMES COMEY – ABSOLUTELY NO LOYALTY

4

CHAPTER 5

JAMES COMEY
A REAL LACK OF LEADERSHIP

We got another good chapter for you today folks and I'm glad you're reading James Comey Absolutely No Loyalty. In this chapter we're talking about James Comey being a real lack of leadership... I was hoping I didn't have to respond to. Like everybody already knows that right! There isn't even no point in putting a question mark on that one. Everybody already knows the answer to that one.

Well if not then ah folks ... they say they had James Comey leading the FBI and he shouldn't even have been allowed to lead the Boy Scouts. Yeah, they say it's that bad folks.... I know, and yes. I was thinking the same thing too. When you think it goes from bad to worse, this Comey guys gets terrible folks.

I was watching Hannity on Fox news and you heard he got the inside scoop since him and Trump shared some legal advice with the same attorney Michael Cohen. Or at least their acquaintances or something but anyhow to be honest, I don't know why some people was calling on Fox news to fire Hannity, if anything I was thinking they should pay him more cause he got the inside scoop with Donald Trump and his attorney, right? Inside scoop, pay more?? So, when I heard that I started watching Hannity first cause if anyone's going to get the breaking news out of the White House, it's going to be Hannity first right?

However, like I was saying I was watching Hannity when the news broke about the release of James Comey's memos and I'm here to tell you folks...that there is ground breaking news that Hannity's watchdogs believe there's enough evidence for criminal referral for James Comey Jr. on at least six charges. Because you do know he's James Comey Jr., right? Anyhow, it appears to me like every 18 U.S.C. section in the book was violated. I was trying to get it all for you good folks, but if you want my inside scoop to the White House I have no reason to hide it from you, it's the Hannity Special on Fox News.

But here we go to the good news folks Slippery Shady James Comey will finally be captured and charged with a lot of charges. We're going to try to go through them as I know, and I think the first charge against Comey is:

Abuse of Power 18 U.S.C. section 242.... Here, everybody knows Comey abused his power to meddle in our 2016 election and everything else in between. They got him on the hook for abusing his power and we're going to talk about that a little later folks. The second charge I believe they're talking about is perjury 18 U.S.C. section 1621.... Hey, you heard about all the lying he's been doing, so this perjury charge should come as no surprise.

123

JAMES COMEY

ABSOLUTELY NO LOYALTY

By: Elliott Lew Griffin

He's definitely lied one too many times and this time to the wrong people. So folks, I guess the word on the street is there closing in on him. They say the lies have gotten so bad that he's telling them in large and small epic proportions. I don't know folks, I'm sorry, I don't know what else to say, Comey is disgraced, discredited and disgruntled right now. And I could only imagine he's lying about everything right now because he already knows he's going to jail. I guess that's why he's coming down to the September 30th Senate convention too tell more lies to try to get himself out of it, and or dig himself in deeper. Like they say when you find yourself in a ditch, quit digging folks. Or in this case it's Comey with his foot on the gas and going nowhere fast.

They say Comey should have a criminal referral for violating 18 U.S.C. section 101. So, I recall I don't know about this one and I'm going to try to check on it with Hannity with you, his show comes on in a minute so I'm not goanna be too long. We're going to get the downlow on that one and I'm pretty sure some new stuff is coming out of the White House. So again, we have the inside scoop on two of the alleged criminal charges already, so please stay with me on the rest and just remember your currently reading James Comey Absolutely No Loyalty.

Well folks we got some good news for you... Hannity don't disappoint, here we go, and I didn't even know this, so it's breaking news. We got some breaking news folks. But apparently when Comey created those presidential memos he did so while acting under the color of a government official. Therefore, Comey knew that once he created those memos in his official capacity, they belong to the government. For that reason, they are saying he broke at least three laws when it comes to taking of those memos from the FBI Building.

The first one they're saying he violated is: 18 U.S.C. section 641 and that is theft of government property. They're saying because those memos belong to the government that when he took them from the FBI building that (that) was theft of government property. #WOW

It gets no simpler than that right there folks. Another two-minute trial. Let me look at that again. We have 18 U.S.C. section 641 and that's theft of government property right. So, he created those presidential memos under the color of a government official and therefore in his official capacity. So, if he did it in his official capacity right here it says according to the law that yup, they belong to the government. Yep folks I think that would be an easy one to prove to the jury. And as a matter of fact, some of my other sources are saying that that's another slam dunk case for the prosecution and now they're wondering why he isn't being prosecuted. Some have even claimed for the life of them they don't know, so yeah, I really don't know folks. Your guess is just as good as mine, if not better. But I'll tell you what? He's going to jail for that one folks.

The next Federal law they say Comey violated was it was 18 U.S.C. section 1924(a) which is a similar charge to 18 U.S.C. section 641 and that's for removing classified documents that belonged to the government. My sources say that this theft of government property charge may be a lesser included offense to the charge of removing classified documents. They say that the documents he stole from the FBI building was classified by himself, so there's no dispute in weather they were classified, and he admitted to taking them.

To say the least folks is over for him. My sources say that charge carries about five years alone. They say he'll do under a United States Supreme court case called Cunningham, so that's Cunningham versus United States and he'll get the midterm. I don't know what the midterm is, but it's definitely a prison term, I don't know folks, so it does carry a minimum of five years so I assume Comey's looking at a minimum five years for those charges alone.

The third charge they're alleging Comey violated was 18 U.S.C. section 793 and that charge directly applies to the fact that you shall not leak classified information. And well that's a known fact, right? I mean that's under the oath of I swear to uphold the constitution. Well what more can we say other than we know he admitted to doing that, so yes, he violated 18 U.S.C. section 793 as well. Simply put, the way Hannity put it in his take, since Comey already admitted that the memos were classified (And come on folks we are talking about a memo that alleges wrong doings by the President of the United States of America, so for that reason you know those memos were highly classified right? So please don't let them lie to you that they weren't classified. Those memos were highly classified information and we know Comey leaked them to some professor guy, who in turn leaked them to the press. So, don't worry folks I think they got the professor guy that is going to tell on Comey too. (That Comey gave him the highly Classified information and he leaked it to the

JAMES COMEY

ABSOLUTELY NO LOYALTY

By: Elliott Lew Griffin

press. I'm actually hoping that we press this professor hard to see if Comey knew he was going to leak the information before he gave it to him, but then again Why else would he give him top secret classified information if it wasn't to leak it, right?? Just saying! Please don't be naïve all your life.

But hey, if Comey try to deny I heard they were going to subpoena the professor guy and nab 'em both. The professor guy had to be in on it. They claim he had to have known that those memos were classified and that they have came directly from the government building. Then if that's the case he as 100% in with James Comey to leak our confidential memos and therefore, the professor should be jailed too for aiding and abetting the leaking of confidential governmental information. I don't see why not folks, right? I don't see why not. He was in on it too and should too be jailed for it. He was a professor, he knew better. Anyway, it goes, they got the doctor, they got James Comey and they're both should be going to jail. To be honest I just saw it all on Hannity. Hannity hands down knows folks. He's already explained everything to me and I'm just explaining it again to you just in case you missed the show it was a couple years ago it was a couple years ago now folks. You had to be in on the in a couple years ago so don't worry.

Folks, I'm sorry to have bogged you down with all of this, but I guess if you're against Comey then welcome aboard. We love to have you. These kinds of people think that they can never go to jail, so we finally going to prove to them that they can. And please don't feel bad for him, I think he was the one that was involved in prosecuting Martha Stewart folks and you know

JAMES COMEY

ABSOLUTELY NO LOYALTY

By: Elliott Lew Griffin

America loves her cooking shows. Who doesn't love Martha Stewart cooking shows? I can see why she went to jail, James Comey and them potentially lied to her and tricked her into a confession just like it appears they did with Michael Flynn. So again, it's nothing new folks, it's nothing new.

Like I said in the beginning of this book they're going to be looking into a lot of cases that Comey took. Like I say, my sources say that Comey was holding back info from Donald Trump about who funded the Russian Steele dossier. That's equivalent to withholding favorable evidenced to a defendant which amounts to prosecutorial misconduct. Then they have Comey and his cohorts' lying to the FISA judge or at least withholding favorable information in that case as well. And that's prosecution misconduct as well.

So to say the least a lot of Comey's cases may be looked into for those reasons to see if he's hidden variable information that should have been either Turned over to the defendant and are the court in those cases. i.e., Prosecutorial misconduct. And if anything is found true, my sources say that they will take his lawyer license as well. He brought it on himself folks, so don't feel bad. And again, look who we're talking about. Taking James Comey's lawyer license. I mean when they took Bill Clinton's lawyer license remember after he was found guilty of perjury, or something like that. But I do remember they took his lawyer license for a period of time due to perjury, or something, so I don't know why they don't take James Comey's license for a period or Time of life for all of these offenses. Well again I saw take his lawyers license because to be a lawyer you have to be

JAMES COMEY

ABSOLUTELY NO LOYALTY

By: Elliott Lew Griffin

ethical and we know James Comey is about as unethical as they come. Again, folks he brought it on himself so don't feel bad, don't feel bad for him folks.

The obstruction of justice charges 18 U.S.C. section 1505(a) and 1505(b). Now I don't know too much about that one so I'm going to have to check with Hannity and get back with you on that one folks. Just know that good people are on it. To be honest, I don't know what James Comey was thinking when he created those memos, but they are definitely going to lead to his demise. They have already said that loose lips sink ships, and, in this case, it was Comey's loose lips that's going to sink his own ship. And now he said that he may possibly be a prosecution witness against Andrew McCabe his number two guy in charge so maybe he might get a deal of a lifetime to squeal. Unless McCabe beats Comey to punch and tells on him first. You know how that goes folks, once they all start telling on each other to get the best deal it's a free for all after that. And again, I think that they're going to stop giving the people who tell deals. Why because they were in on the crime 100% so why should they only get 10-20-30% of the time when they were in on the crime 100%. So again, I think the laws are changing on that. Either that are society is. I think they're going to call it the James Comey and Andrew McCabe law if they start telling. One thing for sure, we'll see it all in a minute folks.

For real like wow, you just can't make this stuff up. But hey in any case if Andrew McCabe does come forward and that was the number two guy in charge he might get a deal, unless Maccabeats coming to the punch and tells on him first period we talked about that we will keep you updated because this is an investigation that all Americans should be concerned with and again call me will be on Capitol Hill September 30th so we will find out more information then we'll see you then.

And however, Donald Trump calls it the Witch-hunt, but I call it the Warlock hunt. I guess it's the same thing other than one's male and the other female. But I don't know, who am I right. Well at least I'm not James Comey who talks about a man's hand size, shoe size and tan lines, especially out in the open for the public to hear. So, like I say, please don't quote me on that one folks. I was just thinking of the rationale of the term witch hunt, but I don't think any females was in the hunt. So again, I don't know folks, it was James Comey's book. He was the one talking about man's hand size, shoe size and tan lines folks, so I don't know. I'm really sorry and at this point all I can say is please keep reading...

JAMES COMEY – ABSOLUTELY NO LOYALTY

COMEY

YOU SHOULDN'T HAVE DONE YOUR BOOK TOUR

CHAPTER 6

JAMES COMEY
NOT CREDIBLE

We got another good chapter for you good folks and it's unfortunate that there's a lot of bad folks. I definitely appreciate you staying with us and reading James Comey Absolutely No Loyalty> I appreciate that thank you. And please tell your friends or tell anybody you know we're on to corruption folks.

What we got another good one for you today, you might want to fasten your seatbelts, you're in for a wild ride on this one folk. We're going to try to get it all to you and I'm going to tell you right now it's a lot and when I say lot, I mean it's a whole lot. Here we go I just hope you got your seat belt buckled because we checked with Hannity in a special edition and I don't know why [WE] did that folks, it's all bad.

I see why they pay him $29,000,000 a year because he's onto uncovering corruption, folks. So far what we know is that the deep state is under siege, it's all bad. I guess Comey's blatant lies

JAMES COMEY

ABSOLUTELY NO LOYALTY

By: Elliott Lew Griffin

still continue and they just said today he's just not credible whatsoever period. From what I hear he's in serious legal trouble and others has said he's in very very hot water. You know that at 211 Degrees Fahrenheit water is hot, so from what I know Comey is in the 211 degree range right now and that sounds about right because 211 is a robbery and in 2016 he definitely robbed us of our democracy here in America. But I'll tell you what folks, at 212 degrees Fahrenheit water boils, so from what I gather they got Comey in the water like a lobster and the water is heating up on him as we speak. Before he knows it, the water is going to start boiling at 212 degrees, then you already know what happens after that folks, he's going to be cooked, if he's not already.

To put in blatant term's folks, James Comey is in serious legal trouble. He's deceived Congress and the America people. Everything that he's done a date has now backfired on him. And now he's under some serious criminal legal investigations because of it. They stole seven documents from the FBI building and at least four of them was highly classified top-secret government information. According to my sources at least two of the documents he leaked to his professor friend at Columbia University were highly classified. I think they're going to file criminal charges on the professor as well. My sources say they also got the professor on the hook for aiding and abetting James Comey and leaking confidential government information. Really, it's just all a mess and I think they're all going to jail. They said that the professor might flip on Comey if he has to testify against.

JAMES COMEY

ABSOLUTELY NO LOYALTY

By: Elliott Lew Griffin

Like I say, don't worry folks, we're going to get to the bottom of it. We're going to get to the bottom of it folks. Right now, my sources say that James Comey will be on Capitol Hill come September 30th, 2020, so again folks we shall see what happens at that time.

Check with Hannity and the DOJ's investigating Comey's memos as we speak. I also found out that the Digital Watch is suing the DOJ over Comey's and Mueller communications. Everybody knows who Mueller is right? Robert Mueller the special counsel that was investigating the Russian Hoax folks. Anyhow. Like they say, they're claiming that since Mueller and Comey are friend's entire corruption thing going on in the government. They're claiming they called me, and Miller are best friends and Mueller knows that called me is corrupted Millers not investigating him because commies his friend. That we need a special second prosecutor to investigate the FBI, especially since Mueller was also the head guy in charge of the FBI at one point or something like that. Indo know that Robert Mueller was a high ranking official of some kind and his cronies we're none other than James Comey. Now I know that for sure.

Like I said folks I don't know, I told you to buckle your seatbelts because the corruption is going deeper. They said Comey is a prosecutor that's prosecutor people and now going to be prosecuted. They say Mueller's an investigator that's been investigating people and now he's going to be investigated as well. I told you folks it went from bad, to worse, to terrible and now where to the unbelievable. I hate to hit you with the next chapter, but from what I hear it's going to get a whole lot worse before it gets better. They're onto them folks just know that. There on to them.

They also want to know how James Comey was able to use all the ongoing criminal investigation evidence in his book A Higher Loyalty. From what I hear he was not to use none of that evidence in his book because it was specific information the public should not have been privileged too. They say they also are looking into investigating Mueller because they believe that he may have given Comey permission to use that confidential information in his book. So I don't know if Comey paid Mueller for permission to use that information, or he gave him permission because their friends, and or Comey just went rogue again and used the stolen top secret government information to sell his book on his own. I guess they're going to get down to the bottom of all of that as well when they talk to Comey and Mueller because Comey did use some kind of classified information in his book for a higher royalty.

From what I gather that's why the Judicial Watch is suing the DOJ for them to turn over all of Comey's and Mueller's communications. I don't know folks, I guess Mueller was once the head of the FBI and Comey was once the head of the FBI too, so for that reason they are saying that they may not be able to trust neither one of them. You know the phrase back to blue, back the blue. Well I guess they have a thing going on talking about back the FBI, back the FBI, and I guess back the FBI mean they support a full coveruption campaign. But hey we have James Comey at the top of the FBI and what does he do, he blows it. Our number two guy Andrew McCabe, top FBI official, again

JAMES COMEY

ABSOLUTELY NO LOYALTY

By: Elliott Lew Griffin

blows it. The number one guy went down, the number two guy went down and now we should be on the lookout for the number three guy. I know there are a lot of men and women in FBI that put their lives on the line to save ours every day and that's sad that I heard they too are mad at this investigation. All of this corruption is just destroying the FBI image The FBI's name and the amazing People it supports. It's just too bad, those rotten apples always try to spoil the bunch, and I hate when they do succeed.

Now I know they've already taken a lot of criticism for dropping the ball on several tips about the Marjory stoneman Douglas High School shooter and if that wasn't disheartening, we are now faced with yet more corruption and scandals coming out the FBI. They say corruption at the FBI is at all time high and they think they believe they found the serial leakers and they're trying to get a handle on the rest of the scandals.

That's why I'm goanna tell you folks, that if you see something suspicious, please don't call the FBI, call the CIA. Seriously, there is a lot going on within the FBI right and we still haven't seen if anyone got fired or reprimanded for dropping the ball on the Marjory Stoneman Douglas shooter tips. They say there's was several tips coming out of Florida about this school shooter and the FBI failed to follow up on the tips. Had they done so, that horrific school shooting could have been prevented. At this point it's hard to say whether or not that's true, but what's true is we know the FBI received tips about this school shooter and never once acted upon them. Now we got the FBI that can't be trusted, the Police can't be trusted. The politicians can't be trusted. I'm telling you right now we're looking a little grim or bleak right now when it comes to having a higher moral standard. And the crazy part is our moral standard is down and our morale standard is down too. Now how bad is that, really? At this point it's almost like we're disgusted and can't be trusted.

And I'm - I'm sorry folks, I hate to say it like that. Why? Because I hate to talk about my country, but we gotta do what we got to do to keep us safe here in America. If the FBI wants to gain our public trust again, they got to start telling on each other to end all the corruption that's going on in that Bureau. The same with the police departments. It seems like they're all crooked. Now with the current Mueller-Comey communications probe, it's really going all bad folks. I wouldn't be surprised to see if President Trump's orders the CIA to raid Mueller's office to get his communications, but call me before he has a chance to destroy them because my sources say that Mueller gave Comey the permission to use the top secret classified information is book. Well like they say, if he did, they are all going to jail folks. They're all going to jail. I don't know folks they keep saying Mueller's office might get raided. Mueller's office might get raided

.   I'll tell you what? I'll keep checking on Hannity with the updates of this investigation cause I believe he'd be the first to know if Mueller is going to hand over his communications or if they're going to go in there with a search warrant to get them. To be honest, I don't know if I'm supposed to be telling this information to the public cause it might give Mueller a warning to get rid of it before they go in there and get it. So right now all I can do is give you a quote from Conan Doyle which says: "It's a wicked world, and when clever man turn their brains to crime, it is the worst of all". I know folks, all I can say is this is an investigation like no other period. I don't think that there has ever been a high corruption scandal like this in the Edgar J. Hoover FBI Building at least modern-day history. Today it seems like we have the lead investigator investigating the investigated and then the investigator is being investigated by the Judicial Watch dogs. I guess that's why we have the Judicial Watch dogs and I would like to just thank them for the work that they're doing here with this James Comey show. They're keeping them fair and honest folks and if Mueller is giving Comey slack or special treatment cause they're FBI friends, then I believe they'll find that out as well.

I know you might not believe all of this folk but come on you can't make this stuff up. Especially since there's even more. I warned you to fasten your seat belt because we were going on an unbelievable ride and I'm going to try to slow the ride down for a second and give you a little good news, so all of the bad news just doesn't overwhelm you. I know the corruption is at all time high and I don't want you to run out on me folks because I need you on the front line. So hey, please keep reading and please bear with me you're reading...

JAMES COMEY – ABSOLUTELY NO LOYALTY

5

ALL CHAPTER 7

JAMES COMEY
ALL BAD FOLKS

Like I said, before I give you more bad news, I'm going to try to give you some good news folks. I know folks, the corruption in our government is all bad, but I will tell you that the world is getting a little more safer as North Korea has announced that its going to be stopping its nuclear weapons and long range ICBM weapons program. They are also closing their nuclear weapons testing sites, so that is great for America folks. Of course, that was a couple years ago, and we still don't have an agreement with North Korea. I know negotiation talks have stalled to some degree, so like I say about everything else, we shall see.

I would say we owe the Trump administration a lot of credit along with other world leaders of the United Nations because they have effectively used diplomatic sanctions against North Korea that is appearing to work. And or that was different from what we used in the past. From what I hear that the economic sanctions that are in place by all world leaders, specially China, the North Koreans biggest ally have devastated the North Korea's economy to the point that it was sadly alleging soldiers were stealing food from the farmers. However, I think Kim Jong Un would give up his nooks and I hope in return the Trump administration and the South Koreans scale back to North Korean missile drills in a sign of good faith that we seek peace and not war.

Again, folks while I have added to this story please be aware that most of this book was written A couple years ago when James Comey published his. Actually, I saw the title and went hell no, later that day I picked up the pen and started writing James Comey – Absolutely No Loyalty. So, like I say, since then all of that has went downhill of course. North Korea has not abandoned their nuclear weapons program. And the Trump administration did stop the Korean missile drills in a sign of good faith that we seek peace and not war, but have yet to come too an official agreement with North Korea that would end the hostility between them and South Korea.

But onto some more good news that might not be good news anymore before we get back to all bad Slippery Shady James Comey show. I found in the course of uncovering all corruption that the Wells Fargo bank has officially admitted to auto loan abuse and that it unnecessarily sold auto insurance to thousands of its auto loan customers. This has caused you the people to fall behind on larger than usual car payments and defaulted on your loans which caused your car to be repossessed. So if you had auto insurance or a car loan through Wells Fargo that you paid higher payments on or your car was repossessed, then they owe you folks a lot of money and or a new car. Like they say Wells Fargo has cheated people out of a car due to inaccurate higher payments so if you were cheated folks please get your money back. Get your money back America.

Also with the same bank Wells Fargo in a separate case, they also admitted to forcing you good people the customers to pay unnecessary fees to locked in mortgage rates, so folks they admitted to that as well. Therefore, if you had a house or business mortgage rate that they were making you pay unnecessary fees for, please go back and get your money back America, and or if you lost your house please go back and get it back from Wells Fargo folks. They have been cheating people for a long time and they finally got caught. They had to pay a billion dollars folks and they might still be screwing people. Like I always say if Wells Fargo is willing to cheat you today folks, they will be willing to cheat you tomorrow too. Like I always say do yourself a favor folks if wells Fargo's cheating people then guess what, close Wells Fargo down. How can you close Wells Fargo down by just closing your bank account. They will get the message. Now if you do that, they might go on cheating more people because they're going down, but hey, at least they won't be cheating you anymore right folks. And like I say, they're cheating people so pull your money out fast folks, pull your money out fast.

Anyhow they owe you good folks' money and an apology so please don't take no or nothing for an answer. Now if they don't want to give you anything, I would talk to Mick Mulvaney cause he just ordered Wells Fargo to pay him 1 billion dollars in fines,

JAMES COMEY

ABSOLUTELY NO LOYALTY

By: Elliott Lew Griffin

the largest in United States history to apparently the American government. So, I tell you what, I don't see how they can get the money and you don't. Wells Fargo got all this money and they still want to juice all you good folks out of yours. I don't know what kind of people think like that, but you might want to think about changing banks folks. They cheat you or your neighbor, or anybody out of their house and their car that's corruption folks. And please whatever you do don't support corruption today folks, please don't support corruption today. People go to work every day and work hard only to get cheated out of their hard-earned assets by none other than stinking Wells Fargo. Yeah OK.

Like Franklin D. Roosevelt said: "We must be the great Arsenal of democracy" and I'll tell you what if we stand by and let them cheat people out of their money and their transportation, then what's going to stop them from doing that same thing to one of us the next time. Therefore, get your money back America, get your home back America get your car back America. Wells Fargo has held on to it for far too long. Get your stuff back today and or make them pay for what they cheated you out of that day.

To be honest if Mick Mulvaney knew about the Wells Fargo corruption, then they knew exactly wo everybody was that Wells Fargo cheated, and guess what, they didn't notify you. They didn't say nothing. They got a Billion Dollars from Wells Fargo and the People that got cheated got nothing, but a loss of their car and house.

And this is my last paragraph on this car and home deal with Wells Fargo, so if you've been affected please listen. Don't take no for an answer. If you have any problems out of Mick

JAMES COMEY

ABSOLUTELY NO LOYALTY

By: Elliott Lew Griffin

Mulvaney call your local Congressman. If you Congressmen or Congresswomen won't help you tell them, you will not be voting for them next time. That's for sure. They lost your vote and tell everybody you know not to vote for them no more too. Tell me and I won't vote for me either. Whatever it is folks make sure you get paid from Wells Fargo. Like I say Mick Mulvaney got 1 billion dollars from Wells Fargo folks so please go get your money back folks. Thank you!

Well sorry folks, I might have to turn you back to your regular schedule reading of Mr. it's impossible himself, Yes, Slippery Shady James Comey. Yeah, I know folks, he has absolutely no loyalty. Now I know you probably don't want to hear no more, but I'm here to tell you what they say and that is that the crimes that James Comey have committed constitutes acts of treachery to you the American people. I believe that because Comey's been alleging that he committed this crime for you folks. Honestly, I don't know what kind of defense that is, but I do know that we the American people can't let him get away with blaming his crimes on us, that's for sure. I know one thing for sure that's not making sense folks and that's, not only has he gotten away with his crimes so far, but it has been reported from another source not Hannity on this one that Comey has sold over 1 Million books

I'll tell you what, that fact is all bad for our democracy. It's just showing a really bad example to a lot of people that they can do Bad things, commit crimes, steal top secret information from the government and get away with it. Now is that Peter struck book starting to sound a little bit more familiar to you. We must stand up America and say #Not today!

JAMES COMEY

ABSOLUTELY NO LOYALTY

By: Elliott Lew Griffin

Right now, I'm going to give you a quote from Solon 6 century B.C., so this quote has been around a long-time folks. You may have heard it, but if not it says: "Laws are like spider webs if some poor weak creature comes against them, it is caught but a big one can breakthrough and get away". Here, we can't let Slippery Shady James Comey get away folks. Like I said, we got to stand up and say #Not today. They have gotten away with this kind of corruption for far too long and the crazy part is they know, they've prosecuted people like Martha Stewart for the same thing? They know. Then for the audacity of Comey to say that he committed his crimes in the name of us the American people, like come on we can't let him slip away with that one. I'm sorry but Comey you did not commit your crimes in my name, so quit saying that because I'm American and real Americans aren't buying it today. Like I say, so sorry but not today.

Then I heard what my inside sources reported and that was him and the lead investigator Robert Mueller are friends. Of course, we talked about that and they say that might be the reason that he's not currently being prosecuted. Now I don't know how true that is, but that's a story for another time folks. Not to mention the fact that Mueller may have given Comey permission to use the top-secret information in his book, so again I believe that they are going to do an investigation into both of them.

To say the least we're going to eventually find out folks, like I say we eventually found out about the Russia investigation and it was all a hoax folks. I know if they don't give us the information or try to hide it from us, I believe those in charge will order them to kick in their doors and go and get us the information. Like they did to Michael Cohen and Paul Manafort's door. So I'll tell you what? I'm going to stay tuned with Hannity folks cause if anybody knows they're going to go up in there and get it...it's going to be Hannity. I guess it's like Lord Action said: "Power tends to corrupt and absolute power corrupts absolutely". Well I guess you're watching that here now. The James Comey Absolutely No Loyalty show.

All I can say is maybe Comey feels that since Mueller is his friend, he has absolute power to continue his corruption, but I think the American people is too upset right now to let him get away with it. I know every American wants to know the truth and I'm trying my best to give it to you right here and right now.

I know it's like what Aristophanes has said "You should not decide until you have heard what both have to say". Well with Comey you have heard from both the left and the right and to say the least they have both expressed they're against him to some degree. The left is a little less so because they want him to tell on Donald Trump, but the truth is Comey doesn't have anything because he was fired 100 days into Trump's Presidency. To be honest, the way it's really shaping out with the release of Comey's memos that Donald Trump can end up being a witness against Comey.

Then of course there's Comey's side, but what he's saying isn't making sense, especially his claim that he committed his crimes for us the American people. I know it may appear like I'm biased cause I've already said I'm 100% partisan against Comey, and

JAMES COMEY

ABSOLUTELY NO LOYALTY

By: Elliott Lew Griffin

that's the truth I am 100% partisan against Comey, but here's why I say that....

I said that because the truth and nothing, but the truth is partisan. If the truth were bipartisan it would be a lie, right? With truth, you either have 100% truth or you have 99. 8 or 99.9 percent, it's just not 100. Everybody knows that 100% is the truth. 99.8 is not now the error proof test. 99.9% might pass Constitutional muster but 99.1 is a radio station and it will definitely not hold up to 100% of the TRUTH RIGHT?

Here, we have concrete evidence that I presented to you and that Hannity's been telling you for years that James Comey should be jailed for the crimes he committed, and that's 100% the truth. That's why I say I'm partisan folks because there is no in between when it comes to corruption, it's either 100% you violate the law, or you didn't. So, I'll let you be the judge of that, but I'll tell you what, don't let them fool you folks. Don't let James Comey fool you folks. He is a crook. Why? Because he stole confidential information memos from the FBI Building. His workplace. And personally, leaked them to his friend. Corruption at it's finest and he should be jailed for it.

Just think if the bank Wells Fargo had gotten away with their scandal, they would still be overcharging people, knowingly taking good people's homes and cars, and not even caring about its folks. They only seem to care when they get caught. (Remember that!) You see Comey's running around smiling and laughing in all his interviews and late-night TV shows. Not caring that he knowingly meddled in our 2016 presidential election. Not even caring that he stole confidential information from the

FBI building. And a whole host of other things that he doesn't even care about and we just let him walk away again Scott free.

To be honest if you ask me folks, I believe James Comey has committed one of the biggest abuses of power scandals in United States history by knowingly interfering in our 2016 presidential election. We should not let him get away with it because his friend is one of the leading investigators that we had investigating this entire hoax. It's all bad folks, James Comey is all bad and with that I'm going to leave you with a quote from Learned Hand and it says: "Liberty lies in the hearts of men and women; when it dies there no constitution, no law, no court can save it at all". So with that said, all I can say is please don't let Liberty die with you and if you want to know more, please keep reading...

JAMES COMEY – ABSOLUTELY NO LOYALTY

6

CHAPTER 8

JAMES COMEY VIOLATED ALL FBI PROTOCOL

I know folks, the deeper we're getting into this the more serious it's getting, or to be honest, I was serious the whole time and I think you're starting to realize it. I'll tell you this Comey strikes me in his interviews as a man of above average intelligence, to us his characterizations against him, so we know he knew what he was doing and all I could say is his lies are all catching up to him. Like I've said before, the truth has got his boots on and Comey it's here for you.

Now I know I heard many people say that if they were Comey, they would cancel the book tour, but clearly, I don't think he's going to period. To me, it's one or two, greed or he feels he's really untouchable.... Either way we got to get him folks, we got to get him folks. One thing for sure, him and McCabe stories diverge, so one got to roll over on the other eventually. So like they say, eventually one will tell on the other. You know how it go. When one starts telling on the other the other starts telling back. Therefore, we know that there is a trap laid out their folks. We all know Andrew McCabe told many lies and he just prosecuted Michael Flynn for illegally doing the same thing, but then we all see how the Michael Flynn case has turned out and I believe Andrew McCabe was involved in that as well. So again, we all know he knew what he was doing, and he must have knew he could potentially be going to jail.

Hey what can I say, these people roll over on each other all the time. For real, that's what they when they get in trouble. They start telling. People start going to jail. And they seem to get a deal and walk away every time. I'll tell you what we're going to get James Comey in the hearing. We're going to get Andrew McCabe in the hearing. We're going to get the law professor that James Comey leaked the information to in the hearing. And after that we will come to a conclusion that they were all involved in the mishandling of information with the FBI an involved in clear corruption on an epic scale. And for you folks that super sad. Come on now we're talking about the head FBI director number one guy James Comey. Then we're talking about the #2 guy Andrew McCabe all at the same time go bad. Like I say folks our next question should be where is the #3 or the number 4 guy in line to the FBI.

And that's why I have said, how are half half-truths, not considered whole laws. How's his explanation for everything he did not viewed as whole eyes? To me if you tell me one misleading statement in our conversation then I am only left to believe that you are trying to mislead me in some kind of way.

Everything it appears that we asked him of substance has been a lie. Like Sir or better yet Crooked Comey that's not adding up. Why break FBI protocol and his answer didn't add up a little bit. They've been way off and at times even contradictory. Like one side he says politics didn't enter his decision, but then he was looking at the polls when he did it? Then, I'm still at why he broke FBI protocol and he can't explain that. Nor can he explain why he's giving us two or sometimes three different answers to the same questions.

I would say for him to be a former prosecutor and Head FBI Director I would assume that he had a lot of contact with lying criminals. However, he's not that good at lying. I cannot imagine James Comey even coming to me for a head FBI job and I hire him. He has no FBI qualities whatsoever to me. The way he talks, acts, his responses and please forbid his logic, it just screams bonehead incompetence to me.

Then if Comey can sit there and claim he served in the FBI under 3 presidents, then how does he not know FBI policy? As a matter of fact, how is he the head guy in charge of the FBI and he claims to have not known protocol. At every level he broke the rules during the 2016 presidential election and now we're supposed to act like that didn't happen and our accept that it was just a mistake on his behalf. (Yeah okayyy) And we're to do all of that even when it's answers on the same questions are contradictory or not making sense.

JAMES COMEY

ABSOLUTELY NO LOYALTY

By: Elliott Lew Griffin

Like they say yeah OK.... Sounds like he's trying to sell his fried ice cream to Me and if I wanted to buy milk, I'll just buy milk. Did he violate FBI protocol once, he did its multiple times and on several occasions? He did it with the Hillary Clinton investigation, the 2016 presidential election and even with his alleged obstruction of justice charge against Trump where he stole and leaked those memos. So again, we're talking about 3 completely separate incidents that Comey were involved in and all 3 were crimes, right.

Not to mention that he's been claiming in the media for months that he had concrete evidence against Trump for obstruction of justice and when the memos were released, they're actually the number one documents for Trump's defense. Like I said this dude is a habitual liar and for that reason we can't believe nothing he says. Everything he has said so far to date is questionable and I guess that's why he continuously saying, "it's possible", right?

However, what's probable is he's lying that's for sure. He even said that he hasn't heard of Hannity and for him to be in the political arena for quite some time I even find that questionable. Don't worry he's going to hear about Hannity when Hannity keeps calling for the slimeball to be prosecuted, that's for sure. And Hannity almost be screaming on the show to lock James Comey up and come doesn't know about Hannity yeah right. Fox News and James Comey was a stanch Republican.... Like yeah okay. What Republican hasn't heard of Hannity. And I mean he be screaming for Hillary too, but in a sense, he is screaming about all corruption. Maybe not so much about Trump, but the left had been screaming about Russia for years and we haven't seen no evidence of that yet?

Then for Comey to claim he had evidence, OMG on that one I don't know what to say folks? Other then of course, he is a staunch liar. In one of his memos he said he pledged loyalty to Trump, but in his George Stephanopoulos interview, he said he only pledged honesty. There are just lies all over the place and I know if I would have read his book, I probably would have concluded there were a lot more lies. I still can't get past the title A Higher Loyalty. Like yeah okayyy....

Slippery Shady James Comey, the greatest threat to our democracy folks. Then in another one of Comey's memos he claims Trump wasn't at all concerned with the fact that the Russians tried to interfere in our elections, but if I were trump, I would have been looking at him. He got some nerve to talk about someone interfering in our election, and yet he did it twice literally. Then to boot, I still say it was three times more interference than any Russia even had the intent to do, and or was capable of pulling it off.

Everything this dude wrote and said in those memos are pretty much a lie. Crazy part is Comey's memos even proved he never felt obstructed by trump. The whole obstruction of justice allegation against Trump has been a hoax from the beginning. I mean I've been really critical of Trump in my other books, but to find out that this was all a hoax at Comey's expense makes a mockery out of our democracy.

JAMES COMEY

ABSOLUTELY NO LOYALTY

By: Elliott Lew Griffin

Comey in another one of his memos said he wanted to go after leakers, and yet we find out he's the serial leaker. #Wow! Then what makes matters worse, is he leaked FBI classified documents to a third party which proves is intent of leaking secrets to third parties all along. I bet you had he not got the whistle blown on him, he would have never come clean, just like the Wells Fargo Bank, they will still be doing it.

I know earlier in this book I alleged Comey may have written those memos after he was fired, but now I guess they have two witnesses saying that they were in the room when at least one was written. A Dana Boente? And on another occasion this other former FBI Supervisory Special Agent Josh Campbell, that Don Lemons had on his show. When Mr. Lemons asked him the question if he was in the room when Comey had written one of the memos? I'm going to be honest folks; he went really quiet on us after his real meek yes. Then what was really interesting was when Don asked him to elaborate on it, he looked nervous, took off his glasses and appeared to be lying to me folks. Now I'm not a trained pathologist, but the way he removed his glasses appeared like he was lying cause after he was done, he put them back on. That's all I know. After that I said yeah, I see now why he had former in his FBI title too. In any event, the memos don't add up to Jack diddly squat, and I use those words gingerly because they've been lying to us this whole year. To me it's been nothing but a lying scandal and now that I get a real taste of Comey in his interviews, I see why people on both sides actually dislike this dude.

I'm sorry to say that folks, you can't make this stuff up. Come on, James Comey is really that bad. This is more than a catalog of mistakes on Comey's behalf. If anything, this is a catalogue of corruption on Comey's behalf. Many of which he needs to come clean and own up to. That would be the day, right? Then he never explained to us why he revealed Hillary's info and not Trump's info and why he violated FBI protocol on it all to begin with. Again, referring to the 2016 presidential election that he threw against us the American People at the end.

I don't know folks; we're still trying to get to the bottom of this. I tell you I've been working on this day and night trying to get this book to you as soon as possible, so please bear with me hey please keep reading....

JAMES COMEY – ABSOLUTELY NO LOYALTY

COMEY

WE'RE GOING TO ARREST YOU QUICK

CHAPTER 9

JAMES COMEY
ALL FICTION

Well folks, I'm glad to see you're still reading James Comey even though I know you found out he's all fiction folks. And have Absolutely No Loyalty whatsoever. Now I know the last couple chapters were kind of hectic and I was hoping I didn't lose you. Everything has been going a little crazy around here and we're going to try to get to the bottom of all of this, but I'm going to tell you right now folks, you haven't heard everything yet. You know when I told you it had gone from bad to worse to terrible to unbelievable and now focus, because I'm sorry to tell you that we finally made it to the unfathomable

I hate to tell you all that and raise your blood pressure all the way up, but there is a lot more we got to tell you. I'm sorry don't kill the Messenger, but yeah, it's that bad....

I guess we got new details that the Slippery Shady James Comey is on the move to try to pull the wool over your eyes

JAMES COMEY

ABSOLUTELY NO LOYALTY

By: Elliott Lew Griffin

again folks. The word on the street from my sources everything he's saying is fiction folks. They say if you see him and he begins talking, just cover your ears cause it's all lies folks. They say he's out there turning our democracy into a hypocrisy. Have you seen him on T.V. folks...? I heard one of his interviews, don't do it, don't do yourself like that folks?

Last I heard they told him that he might want to pull the plug on his book tour before everything goes South. I guess he's still out there lying folks. Talking about the top-secret documents that he stole from the FBI weren't classified. I know, he was the one that wrote classified on them when he wrote them and now, he's trying to cover it up on his book tour. However I'll tell you this again folks, that if you have a meeting with the president United States and then you're taking notes of what he says in a confidential meeting, then that's already classified information. And actually, that document is highly classified folks. Trust and believe that classified document doesn't mean just aliens or UFO sightings folks.

So trust and believe Slippery Shady James Comey knows that the document he stole from the FBI building were highly classified information and I don't know why he's running around trying to tell you good folks that they weren't classified when they were. That's why he got the name Slippery Shady James Comey folks cause he's trying to slip in a lie anywhere he can. He's trying to throw shade over a lie anywhere he can. But I'm here to tell you folks you all know he's lying. He stole those classified documents from the FBI building and he also been trying to tell the people that since he was the one that created

JAMES COMEY

ABSOLUTELY NO LOYALTY

By: Elliott Lew Griffin

them he had a right to take them, but of course we know that's not true. Once he created those memos in his official capacity then those memos belong to us our government, they don't belong to Comey they belong to the government. And Comey knows that. That's why when he was done drafting them, he did what with them? He logged them into the FBI Building right? Because where did he steal them from? The FBI Building right? So, he knows and please don't let him act like he doesn't and or try to play U.S. like we're all stupid.... Our Politicians might be, but we're not right!

But like I said again, he didn't take those memos home folks and that's because they belonged in the FBI building, they didn't belong at his house. They didn't belong in his possession. They belonged at the FBI Building stored in the Confidential file folder. So yes, he stole them. I guess that's why they say if Mueller doesn't turn over his notes about his meetings with Comey then they're going to get in and get them. And we're talking about real Patriots folks. My sources say that they are really mad that Comey used some of that highly classified top-secret information in his book and they want to know who told them he could use it. Again, I guess we will find that out on September 30th if those in charge has enough mental capacity to ask the right questions. And not let it turn into an outright Kavanaugh hearing.

To be honest I think they're going to pin Mueller and Comey against each other and all else fails somebody is going to tell on somebody. It works every time. Some other sources are saying that McCabe may tell on them all. I don't know folks from what I hear they are going to be calling Comey back to Capitol Hill to testify. Of course, we know that now is September 30th. A lot of his answers on his book tour aren't adding up to what he told them already and then like I said Congress is mad because they know he interfered with our 2016 presidential election. And like I explained in the last chapter he violated all kind of FBI rules and protocols and everything else in between folks, so I really don't know what to say other than hey James Comey will be back on Capitol Hill to testify on September 30th and on September 30th he might go to jail folks....

So yeah folks come September 30th, 2020 we're going to come back and see what's going on and talk about finally locking up Comey for you folks. Already know it's going to be a special edition on Comey because he's going to be the hot topic in the main news cycle so I guess we will wait and see if he keeps lying right? They are onto him and we are onto him too, so don't worry folks, we're gonna catch this slimeball once and for all.

Like I say, don't worry folks, just know that we have some good Patriots onto him. We got to fight the good fight. We got to fight for our principles and our rights; and you know us real Patriots, we take the malicious leaking of our top secret classified governmental information seriously. Even if Comey just made it up himself. I'm sorry it's just that real. That serious folks, the people aren't playing with that. If Comey had stolen some non-classified information, they might let that slide, but now they know he stole classified information and leaked them through a third party, they're really mad about that. I mean come on he is the top official of the FBI and he stole from FBI building and leaked it. Like my sources say that bad precedence. So, hey

JAMES COMEY

ABSOLUTELY NO LOYALTY

By: Elliott Lew Griffin

they're going to have Comey back on Capitol Hill to question him more about all of this on September 30th and if he lies this time, I believe it's over form. They might take him out in handcuffs right then and there before he slips or tries to slip out the front door and or back door. Like I say please don't forget he was the Top Guy at the FBI, so yes he does have clearance to go out the back and get in the helicopter and fly away if your not paying attention.

My new sources say that they've waited until Comey's book tour was done so they could gather all of the questions, and all of his answers (I mean lies), so that they could really get to the bottom of all of his words right. He's said so many and now they have to go in and figure out what's true and what's not. Then I'm pretty sure he's going to face tough question of who, when, where and why someone gave him permission to use the information in this book. And I'm telling you folks, these people are real Patriots and going to take this real serious.

I don't think his buddy Bob Mueller can bail him out of this one. They're going to hire another special counsel who's going to investigate Comey, McCabe and the entire FBI Department. Then this might open up in a Pandora box and come back to bite everybody in the. But seriously folks this is that bad. They already got the number two guy Andrew McCabe because he wasn't as Slippery as the Masterminded Slippery Shady James Comey, but again don't worry folks they're closing in on Comey as we speak. Then if Robert Mueller was in on not turning over favorable evidence that he may have uncovered during his 2 he may have uncovered during his 2 ear investigation that would

JAMES COMEY

ABSOLUTELY NO LOYALTY

By: Elliott Lew Griffin

have led to the prosecution of James Comey then he's going down too folks. It's called obstruction of justice. I don't think he could protect Comey much longer folks. James Comey has just done too much at this point. Therefore, a second special counsel is needed. And or just try him and convict him. I'm not a prosecutor and I bet I get a jury to convict James Comey by the end of the day as long as Comey's defense doesn't take up the whole day. Now that would be a bad day. Having to sit there and listen to Comey lie in trial all day. Like make it stop please. The next thing I'll be doing a Comey sketch and everything of my own. Drawing him with devil horns and everything. The ad-lib bubbles appearing like they're coming off the page. Talking about lie...liess...liesss...liessss...and...more liessss!

Don't worry good Folks my sources say they are keeping a keen eye on the number three guy in FBI as well. I'm going to be honest though.... His Name is Christopher Wray and he too has a little shady look I'm telling you that today. His nonverbal communication character isn't all that great. To say the least something appears a little on the crooked Rudy Giuliani kind of shady look to me, but I could be wrong. However, I am an expert in non-verbal communication, but I'm not a certified expert in non-verbal communication, so I could be a little off, but definitely not far off. That's for sure! Read the title you'll see folks!

You know they got that saying and I don't know who said it first but it says: "That if something happens once then it can only happen once, but if something happens twice then it may surely happen a third". That's why they're keeping an eye on the number three guy right now folks. I'm pretty sure they figured that it happened once under Comey. (Actually, it was like 5 times under Comey, but who's counting right!) Twice under McCabe and they're not going to let it happen again with the number three guy or is this the number 4 guy and #5 guy I don't know folks we're going to find out. Like they say Peter struck just wrote a book, so I guess we're expecting a book from Andrew McCabe any day. Then hey everybody's waiting on the Michael Cohen tell all book on Donald Trump probably. James Comey writing another book Saving Justice. But then again, maybe the Senate will save justice and lock him up before he could publish that book and tarnish our image even more.

Like I said folks, they should seriously be looking into this especially since it was the FBI that dropped the ball on the Marjory Stoneman Douglas High School Shooter Tip. So, before the Marjory Stoneman Douglas High School shooting took place on Valentine's Day 2018, the FBI was apprised with several tips on that shooter and of course they did nothing. I guess the saying goes they were to involved in doing corruption then solving corruption at that time. I mean come on how much more are we going to let them drop the ball on us. This whole thing has just been a flat-out catastrophe. It has cost us many lives and quite frankly bad for the entire country. A lot of people don't know who to trust right now and just the other day I was watching the news and it was a church in Oakland CA that had said that they don't trust police so much that they weren't going to call them no more. Now how sad is that.

JAMES COMEY

ABSOLUTELY NO LOYALTY

By: Elliott Lew Griffin

I don't know what happened in that situation or why they arrived at that conclusion, but if you don't believe me, I'm sure you can Google it? Which church in Oakland CA said they are not calling the police no more? This is getting really sad for America folks, so that's why they keep saying if you see something that looks suspicious and you don't trust the FBI and you don't trust the police who do you call. Like I said folks I guess you got to call the Central Intelligence Agency I don't know folks that's the CIA. Who do you call to come and protect you when you don't who to trust? (I know I get it) And like I say, all else fails just remember the Second Amendment will always be here for you. The Second Amendment will always be here for you.

Now, to be honest, I know we still have a lot of good people in the FBI, I believe we employee some 35 to 40,000 certified FBI Agents, so please try to not let a few bad apples ruin the bunch. We still got some good people working really hard to keep us safe. I don't know how or why they dropped the ball on the Marjory Stoneman Douglas High School case, but I honestly believe other outside agencies are checking into that and once they find who was responsible for that missed tip, we are first going to get it corrected and the person may be fired. You may even be able to Google that and see if they fired somebody on that already. I was at least expecting to hear a PUBLIC APOLOGY for dropping the ball on that one, but okay some random issues statement might work for some people.

I know the #2 Guy Andrew McCabe was in charge during that time and he's been fired already. If I didn't tell you, Trump fired him as soon as the news broke about his corruption. I think I was

JAMES COMEY

ABSOLUTELY NO LOYALTY

By: Elliott Lew Griffin

watching Hannity, because that's my go to guy on all the up to date corruption and I know I saw a tweet that said: "McCabe LIED! LIED! LIED!" And the next thing I knew they reported that Trump fired him (Ha-ha) And it was so funny because it happened just that fast. It was like breaking news and that's why I say I had to be watching Hannity.... Hannity breaking news!

So yeah, I know a lot of people got axes to grind with the president and I got my fair share of gripes as well, not axes folks, not axes. But I will give him credit here because he did our country a great service when he fired both James Comey and Andrew McCabe. That's for sure! I will say that folks. I don't even want to begin talking about Andrew McCabe and everything that he did, but the firing of him was a great service to our country folks, especially since he was in charge of the FBI when the tips from the Marjory Stoneman Douglas High School shooting were missed. So yeah folks he's fired, and I'm glad and now we're just awaiting charges to be fired on him. As already reported here in the criminal referral they sent to the prosecution against him, so we're just waiting on them to finish collecting their evidence and I believe he will be formally arrested here in the near future. I'll make sure to keep checking with Hannity for us and as soon as the information breaks about his arrest and you know I will do my best to try to get that out to you good folks. But again remember, Hannity is my go-to guy. Hannity is my go-to guy. And remember you can go to him too folks, you can go to him too. Fox News...Fox News!

JAMES COMEY

ABSOLUTELY NO LOYALTY

By: Elliott Lew Griffin

As for Slippery Shady James Comey, I Honestly don't know why he turned all bad on us folks, but hey all I can say is stay tuned your reading...

JAMES COMEY ABSOLUTELY NO LOYALTY

'

7

CHAPTER 10

JAMES COMEY REAL SHADY

I guess Slippery James Comey just got a new nickname and it's Slippery Shady James Comey. Now I know you heard it all before, but hey this is where the nickname originated from. Slippery Shady James Comey... I don't know, they are saying he has been acting really really shady lately though, so some have been thinking of changing his name to "Slippery Really Shady James Comey" and or at least "Slippery Super Shady James Comey" who has Absolutely No Loyalty of course, so yes we're going to find out all the facts for you and get them to you as soon as possible. Just know that we're waiting on Hannity to come back because we know he's going to have the new details in the James Comey case, good folks we're onto him.

We are also having to take this James Comey issue to the people and see what kind of answers and feedback we get from them, so we're going to have that for you too. Just know that we're going to round up all the facts for you so you can make

JAMES COMEY

ABSOLUTELY NO LOYALTY

By: Elliott Lew Griffin

your own decision, but so far nothing's been even looking remotely good for James Comey folks.

They keep saying that his interviews are leading to his demise. Then the fact that he scorned both sides aren't helping his case either. I guess some of his new and far in between supporters are just calling on him to just smile & sign books, but I know personally he hasn't been taking that advice so far. All I can say is that he obviously doesn't listen very well and that's probably why he never listened to the FBI when they told him don't talk about the investigation, but my sources say that Congress hopes that he keeps talking because every time he opens his mouth their case against him is getting STRONGER.

All I can say is that he's trying to cash in on this book tour, but it has opened up another whole can of worms. Apparently moderates on the left and the right are still trying to hang in there and support him, but the more they are finding out about him in his interviews, it appears that they are two starting to turn against him. And that may have been his last grasp of defense folks. Everybody knows that the far-right are Trump's people and the far-left are Crooked Hillary's people, so we know they're totally against him, so once the moderates on both sides go, I don't know folks it's "o" simply OVER. Or I guess I do know huh? (Oops)....

I don't know I, that's what I'm hearing from a lot of people is that if Congress or whomever is to hold Comey accountable for his actions cannot let him slip away free, after all the fuss and madness over the ordeal, they know The American People will lose faith and trust in the system, so knowing that I don't believe

JAMES COMEY

ABSOLUTELY NO LOYALTY

By: Elliott Lew Griffin

they are going to allow Comey to slip off the hook . Some say if he would have went away quietly he may have been able to hide in the Shade; while People be out in the beat of the sun looking for him far away, but the writing of the book, the information he used in the book and the entire book tour definitely got Comey back on the hook. But maybe not so much as the book tour, but it was the one-on-one interviews that really got Comey on the hook, and or should I just say greed, because at the end of the day that's exactly what it is we're talking about here today. They claim he shouldn't have done those. And right on que real Patriots are glad he done those. Let's go Patriots…. And don't worry folks we're not talking about New England either and or new English either, sooo You Know Who We're Are. Isn't Elliott THE MAKE AMERICA AMAZING GUY…. Or they must have skipped over that part in the book…(ha-ha)! Made You Look….

But hey we're going to find out folks we are still going to find out, just bear with me because this may be very well the calm before the storm. We are waiting on a lot of new facts about the whole ordeal, all I'm saying right now is Comey's book tour and Andrew McCabe's legal troubles has been sinking the FBI into the ground right now. This is coming at a bad time for them especially like I reported they were the Bureau that dropped the ball on the kids back on Valentine's Day. Forreal, that's disheartening and we still want that Public ("We're Sorry Apology Today) (Now I got two-words for them just like for their weak as school security guard bullet-proof vest wearing non-not even try to shoot the shooter…and it's guess what? (FUCK YOU!) I guess there ain't no guess work in that huh, and ain't ain't supposed to be a word, but for some reason I comprehend it

JAMES COMEY

ABSOLUTELY NO LOYALTY

By: Elliott Lew Griffin

very clearly though. And I'm so sorry Webster doesn't. I should actually come out with my own dictionary. I wonder what it would look like. Gouda anyone? Gouda [Like Youda-Gouda] 1.) "A market town in the Netherlands, just north-east of Rotterdam; population 70,857 (2008); and 2.) Gouda "a flat round cheese with a yellow rind, originally made in the town of Gouda in the Netherlands". That's my dictionary folks, I'm working on it. The word and where it may have originated from.

But hey back to the FBI because like I say, if they missed it and or our guys and gals (our best) were just outsmarted that day, (I could say okay I apologize we TRIED), but to not even follow through on the tip they got, so yes they to take heat from all our Intel Agencies and our Intelligent American People that want to use our Constitutional 1st Amendment rights to tell them the truth about themselves until they "GET THEIR SHIT TOGEATHER!", right?

As far as Comey goes, they say he is on his own and many more can't believe that he would keep putting the Bureau thru all this scrutiny. I think it's the criticism from both sides that' really intensifying the pressure. Like I said, on one side you got your diehard Trump supporters chopping at the bit and on the other you got your diehard Hillary supporters and they're really really mad at Comey for stabbing both of them in the back. Apparently, they are claiming that Comey has had years now and countless hours to think of a possible explanation for what he did during his Crooked Rein as our FBI Director and they're even more mad because his answers aren't even breaking the reason,

172

JAMES COMEY

ABSOLUTELY NO LOYALTY

By: Elliott Lew Griffin

logic or common sense barriers. Some say he's even starting to sound like Joe Biden at times (Incoherent).

I don't know I've been saying the same thing folks. I don't know. I haven't read the book but from the excerpts I heard about it appears like Comey has three separate versions of what's going on. What he originally did. What the book says because of course he probably didn't write most of it and now what his direct answers to the questions that's been asked of him are? And while they have all been changing, the truth is also revealing itself in the process folks. Don't worry James Comey wasn't our only Top Law Enforcement Official. And you know we got some folks - folks. Don't act like you don't know. What they say keep playing and you may even get citizens arrested. Or did they quit doing that when I got arrested. Well folks, what I learned is it's easier to just call the police and let them deal with it. AND WHAT IF THEY DON'T TAKE HIM TO JAIL LIKE THEY DON'T TAKE COMEY TO JAIL??? THEN WHAT DO YOU DO....

I GUESS YOU JUST GOT TO USE YOUR COPING SKILLS AND TURN AROUND AND LET THEM CONTINUE TO SCREW YOU...OR ELSE WHAT ELSE CAN YOU DO RIGHT?

I know I could ONLY imagine FBI detectives all around the world are shaking their heads at this James Comey show. They're trying to uphold their images in their communities as being the upper eslauch of American people and have been riddled with scandal after scandal after scandal, by none other than James Comey.

And see that's what happens when the people at the top go south, the ones below them get viewed the same way. I could only imagine what's going on through many of their minds as they know many Americans are looking at them as part of the corrupt FBI they see on TV. I'm pretty sure somewhere there's people scared to give the FBI information because they may leak it. That's why they say the leaking of the top secret classified information is serious folks. This is not a game, and many are left wondering why COMEY has been able to avoid prosecution all this time, like it's a game. I guess Comey claimed in one of his interviews that he was a no-win situation and many people are thinking with Comey they are in a lose-lose situation. I know his reputation continues to go from martyr to villain and the more he talks, the deeper he's been digging himself and the FBI in a ditch. They have a saying and it is: "If you find yourself in a ditch, quit digging !" , but I'm ASSUMING COMEY has never heard that just like he says he never heard of Hannity..., and or simply doesn't care about himself or the people in the Bureau either. We will see folks, we will see. All I can say at this point is please keep reading ...

JAMES COMEY – ABSOLUTELY NO LOYALTY

8

CHAPTER 11

JAMES COMEY
A REAL WEASEL!!!

Well folks, we got some new information piling in. First Eric Holder our former Attorney General is going down in flames. Apparently, he said that James Comey was a truthful person and a man of Honor and a lot of people aren't liking that, especially after more and more information is coming out about Comey's many lies. Then many have said that Eric Holder's opinion don't even matter cause he's had his own downfalls as being the only Attorney General in the US history to ever be held in contempt of Congress or at least that's one of my sources are saying. Eric Holder was held in attempt of Congress?

I know if that's the truth then yeah, Holder would appear to not be a man of honor or truthful person as well. Man, the only person to ever be held in contempt of Congress in the US history, I see why he still friends and trying to stick up for James Comey. That is a prime example of more birds of the feather flocking

JAMES COMEY

ABSOLUTELY NO LOYALTY

By: Elliott Lew Griffin

together folks, more birds of a feather flocking together... When will it stop, I don't know...? This James Comey is definitely not shaking out to be a good guy I know that to say the least folks, he's officially jumped out of his frying pan and into the fire, if you asked me.

Just avoid him folks, just avoid him. The stuff he's doing is really crazy and I don't want to see you get caught up with him. A lot of people are talking some crazy things about him from the legal trouble side and many more want to burn grass with him, so he's not a man you really want to be around right now.

Apparently, my sources reveal that even Donald Trump may file a defamation of character lawsuit on James Comey for all the lying, cheating, sneaky weasel moves he did to him. In that lawsuit I guess it could be alleged that Comey had spread really bad stories on Trump for about a year about Obstruction of Justice, and Collision with the Comey memos which has all been proven to be false information from the beginning. Now with the Russia Golden shower story that the media is eating up in James Comey's book, Trump may have a case if he was to pursue it and I will report that Comey has the money to pay right now from his book deal.

I know with all of the stuff I put in here about James Comey he may want to file a defamation of character suit against me. I'll tell you what, all the lies he told, I wish he Would I would Michael Avenatti him. Then he'll have to file his claim in the federal court with all the lying and federal leaking he been doing...we're going to be rich folks, with the counter lawsuit claim we file on him. I guess we would throw that out there if he

JAMES COMEY

ABSOLUTELY NO LOYALTY

By: Elliott Lew Griffin

was ever thinking it because he definitely doesn't need my assistance to defame him, he's doing a great job of that on his own folks.

He messed around and got in court and even the judge gave him information talking about how he left stuff out. I could only imagine the persecution having to turn over their evidence to the defense and it would be like what Trump's legal team said about the Comey memos, all of this is Exhibit A comma folks. For real, like exhibit A-Z and we'll be moving on to exhibits 1, 2, 3... with all the crap they got against Comey right now.

If I ever heard them use the phase his goose is cooked again, I know I would look around to see Comey's picture right above it. It's that bad folks it's that bad. The list goes on and on. I guess Comey called Trump "morally unfit" and "a stain" and I honestly don't know why Comey won't leave the Trump people alone because apparently, they're telling Comey "Look Who's Talking".

The Trump people are claiming that Comey was morally and fit to run the FBI especially since he violated almost every FBI moral & ethic code in the book. Then on the top of the lying, he got the theft, and the leaking and to be honest folks it's getting worse. Here, we have a letter to the editor of the New York times dated April 26, 2017 from Elliot Jacobson another (Elliot right), but who was Comey's former colleague who wrote that: "Comey violated every rule in the book governing the conduct of the federal law enforcement officials", so they been knowing about Comey for a long time. I don't know, but if I had to tell the man to leave the trump people alone and just kick back and wait quietly until the people come to arrest him.

JAMES COMEY

ABSOLUTELY NO LOYALTY

By: Elliott Lew Griffin

Maybe that's why he's making such a big fuss because he already knows he's going down. I'm pretty sure you heard about it in your own daily lives. Like make it stop already. I'll tell you what, this may be around in the media for a very long time especially once they file charges on him and God forbid they don't, I can just see people like Hannity screaming about it every day. Just shaking his head in disbelief. I know, I'm going to be right their folks shaking my head in disbelief too. Trying to figure what the Slippery Super Shady James Comey comic book is going to look like. Wonder which comic hero he slips away from first and I don't know about you, but I'm definitely thinking it would have to be Captain America first. Then maybe, I'll have other forces joining in trying to catch him. All I can say is I hope you're interested? Or not right, they know what to do, they know what to do. Probably nothing right? That sounds about right?

Now I know you may hear about me, but I want you to know that I only beat the guy up because he was stealing my stuff and the Police wouldn't haul him away after the 10th time, and I'm really sorry he met me at the 11th hour trying to steal my car trailer that day. Justice just isn't fair and that's why you got to read the facts folks. (I was fighting corruption, and sure in the heck ain't running from it neither) I know ain't ain't ain't word, but like I told you that's only according to Webster…. You might want to start listening to Uncle Elliott because again…still here fighting injustice and corruption right now. We are going to get it right. I hope? To say the least, if we continue to allow injustice, unfairness and corruption thrive in our lives we are in for a world of trouble.

179

JAMES COMEY

ABSOLUTELY NO LOYALTY

By: Elliott Lew Griffin

You see how Comey and his cronies do it, they lie to judges, the People and everybody else in between. Just this time they got caught. Like I say, if they were doing it this late in their career, I could only imagine how much evidence these people have hid from judges and People all over the years. That's why I say these people be the worst of people because they screw people over while still thinking their good, down home decent people. Like come on, really?

However, they're going to jail this time and the American people are going to win on this one. Justice will prevail on this one. The American People are starting to see it for what it is, a big corruption scandal going on in our courts, judicial system, law enforcement and government officials. We got to start holding somebody accountable folks or this problem will never end. It's like the Wells Fargo Bank, they only quit when they get caught. Then all the sudden, their story. Well sorry isn't going to bring them people and their kids home or car back. They didn't care when they were doing it and trust and believe they knew they were robbing people and their children of their homes and their vehicles when they were doing it, right?

James Comey and his cronies know that they've been doing, and they've been doing it for decades. The world only got up on these people because the spotlight was shined on Donald Trump and he just so happened to turn his media attention towards them, otherwise we wouldn't have never Really payed attention to it. Why because nobody cared about Slippery Slopey James Comey and or Lacking Candor Andrew McCabe before Trump, so essentially this is Trump taking down these FBI guys folks. Or

JAMES COMEY

ABSOLUTELY NO LOYALTY

By: Elliott Lew Griffin

should I say the hate Trump media, trying to take down Trump (That did exist at that time). So yeah, I'll confirm that Comey is going to jail for trying to take down the Don....

And like I say I don't know what Comey was thinking, he was the one that said Trump runs his life like a Mob Boss. Well now Comey's going to jail for illegally trying to take down Trump, right? Isn't that what we're talking about. Comey wore a wire or tape recorder to the white house trying to get Trump in trouble. Created these falsified classified Confidential memos against Trump. Then logged them into the FBI Building. Then thought of a devised plan to go steal those documents from the FBI Building and leak them to his friend (who must have been in on it) {And what is he in on, a James Comey Conspiracy to take down the President} {Treason against the Country, if the Crooked Hillary Clinton 2016 election "mistake" wasn't} and now he's lied about everything and hasn't even been arrested, let alone tried and convicted, if he ever will be.

I'm telling you good folks, it's time that we hold these people accountable for what they've done, especially since they must know better, yet still choose consciously to do it. Please believe me that all of Comey's crimes weren't mistakes like he's claiming, they were all deliberate crimes just like he's deliberately trying to deceive you with his lies right now right? And don't worry, he did the same thing to the judge in the FISA Court. That's James Comey he always withholds the truth.

Then he even lied to Congress on the Hill, and got away with it, so if he would lie to them underneath oath, then surely, he has no problem lying to you and me. Hold him accountable folks,

181

hold him accountable. And if you want to know morrreee, please keep reading...

JAMES COMEY – ABSOLUTELY NO LOYALTY

JAMES COMEY
ABSOLUTELY NO LOYALTY
By: Elliott Lew Griffin

COMEY
YOU'RE NOT GOING
TO SLIP AWAY...

CHAPTER 12

JAMES COMEY
A REAL SPEWER

Folks, Comey went from being a leaker to a serial leaker to now the people are saying he's just an outright spewer. I'm sorry I'm just giving you the information as fast as I'm coming across it. They say, everybody in the Southern District of New York knows that James Comey spews more than Niagara Falls folks. Others say that he spews more than the Gulf...so was that the oil burst or the spewing Iraq and Afghan war? Hold on folks, they're currently putting out that he spewed more hazardous material than the Gulf oil spill and they are still trying to clean up that water up folks. Now they are reporting that's a metaphor. But It's just that bad, if not worse folks.

Well I'm sorry to report that our story has gone from bad, to worse, to terrible, too unbelievable, to unfathomable, and finally we just hit catastrophic folks. Just when you thought it couldn't get any worse, we hear this. The crazy part is that I can't even make this stuff up, this is actually what the people are saying and

JAMES COMEY

ABSOLUTELY NO LOYALTY

By: Elliott Lew Griffin

I'm just reporting it to you. This is a major catastrophe. I mean for the people to even link you to those kinds of metaphors; he's got to be spewing folks.

We're going to get to the bottom of this... I'm wondering now why I even signed up for this. I can't take too much more of this myself folks. It's like the scenario of when I just looked out my window and saw the people playing baseball and when the baseball went flying by, all the guy could do was throw the glove at it. I'm telling you that's what I just seen folks, you can't make this stuff up.

I personally don't have a glove right now, but I'm definitely looking over at my towel. The crazy part is we haven't even heard from Hannity or gone out and talk to the people about Comey. At this point the facts are piling on miraculously that it's already taller than Mount Rushmore and at this rate when we're done, all I can say is lookout Mount Everest. I'll tell you what, this is 1 mountain the people may not want to climb. It's so high that there is no oxygen in the air up there, I am flabbergasted. I'm on the ground and it definitely got me looking for a breathing machine just from looking up there......

Yeah, I was thinking the same thing to folks, all I can say is please stay with us. We're going to go out there and talk to some people and then we're going to have Hannity coming in pretty soon, so maybe we can get some good news from somewhere else because I already know the news from Hannity is going to be the death of us. If you got your white flag hold it by your side folks and Please remember your reading....

JAMES COMEY – ABSOLUTELY NO LOYALTY

JAMES COMEY

ABSOLUTELY NO LOYALTY

By: Elliott Lew Griffin

9

CHAPTER 13

JAMES COMEY
NOT A REAL PATRIOT

Hey good folks, I'm sorry. I honestly don't know why I went out there and talk to the people. They mad at Comey folks. We got a bombardment of evidence and I don't know if your hearts can take it. I'm trying folks, but he's looking at some serious consequences.

I don't even know why I signed up for this period. Now I know why he got paid so much for this. You got to have a strong heart to take this. Just give me a second folks just give me a second.

Yeah Comey's image in the public is ruined. Slippery Shady James Comey folks how did yawl let him get this bad. How do the people even know? I'm glad I didn't talk to the no kids. I hope my kids don't know this!

I don't know if yawl want the info folks. I'm sorry to report that this information is so serious we might have to leave it out of his book. Let me think of what Hannity would do? Yeah, I know him, and he would give it to you. Where are the five people

JAMES COMEY

ABSOLUTELY NO LOYALTY

By: Elliott Lew Griffin

at the five when you need them. I don't see their show too often because it comes on over here on the West coast at 2pm. I just mentioned them because I already know it's going to take at least five people in Unison telling you this for you to believe it and you know when one is in agreement with the other four or better yet you know when the other four are in complete agreement with Jesse Waters, you know this is 1 cool story but hey he's Waters and this is his world.

Why did I go ask about James Comey I don't know, your guess is as good as mine? Whatever you do don't go ask about James Comey in your community or even your neighbors around you. Where is Greg Gutfeld when you need him. This is definitely a gut Buster and please just have the ghostbuster go out and get him.

Well from a lot of people that I've talked to they've said that James Comey's not a real Patriot and I'm not talking about the New England Patriots; I'm talking about the American Patriots. So, I went out and I talked to a group of prominently white guys and you could tell they had patriotism, one was even a former marine talking about hurrah. Then I went over and talked to a group of all black guys and they can talk about Colin Kaepernick all they want to but where I'm at you can tell that these black guys really love their country. One black guy said that his family has been real Patriots since the Patriots showed up to save them from slavery during the civil war. I thought like duh, but I really never heard it like that before. It kind of took me by surprise. Then we are in California, this is not Trump territory, but they seem to have a little more respect for Trump after he ordered a

189

JAMES COMEY

ABSOLUTELY NO LOYALTY

By: Elliott Lew Griffin

strike on Syria for gassing its people. Now they said: "don't get too trigger happy", but they showed a lot of pride behind their country for that.

I told you I was going to go out there and talk to the people. We are going to check on Hannity tomorrow to get the full scoop on Comey, but when I told the people I was writing the book James Comey - Absolutely No Loyalty a few of them really thought it was a good idea and went crazy. And I talked to them about Comey being a lying leaking sneaky weasel and they laughed. However, a lot of the aggression towards Comey came from him leaking our top secret classified FBI documents and to say the least these are people that aren't fond of the FBI, and the most dissed hardening thing was how come he leaked the information through a third party you know this isn't really rump land, so they talked about if Comey was going to turn Trump in that he should of told him to his face instead of trying to do it behind his back . I threw out the old war phrase: "Until he seen the whites in his eyes", and they said; Yeah yeah. I egged them on with "eyeball to eyeball", and they said yeah yeah. I then asked them who do you think would have blinked first? They all laughed and said, "Comey fool", "Trump got balls" ha-ha! I thought that was interesting reporting.

However, the gist of it, they all talked about how Comey pledged allegiance to the country not to leak classified information and that it was a disgrace to all of the US in our nation that he did it. I throughout the word "treason" and they ran with it and talked more about how dishonorable Comey was for doing what he did, but I told yawl we got to get him because he said he "was getting paid" for doing it. They were still outraged at the fact that he would do that to our country, and we don't need people like that in the government. To say the least it was interesting and I'm glad I did it. They had throughout the word Coward and that furthered into the phrase "Comey's a Coward" and that I'm going to talk about in the next chapter.

But all in all, I would like to say thank you for bearing with me folks and I'm trying to bring you the best book I can, so with that said, please keep reading...

JAMES COMEY - ABSOLUTELY NO LOYALTY

10

CHAPTER 14

JAMES COMEY
A REAL COWARD!!

I'm sorry I can see right now folks that this chapter is going to be Topsy Turvey. We were hoping to try to start some good chapters, but it's going all bad again. What can I say folks we keep getting more critical cringing information on this Comey character and it's not my fault? I want to start writing some good stuff, but everything we've been receiving on this Comey guy been all bad. It's not my fault. Don't blame me, blame him, at least. It's not me... All else fails blame the government they are the ones that hired him in the first place, and they are the ones that let him get this far out of control. If I was in charge, I would have put an end to this madness a long time ago, so I don't know; I really don't know.

I do know what started all of this Comey talk and that was Comey was talking about how he doesn't like bullies. I don't know why he said that cause everybody's now talking about how Comey's a coward and wouldn't do nothing to a bully. I know at

JAMES COMEY

ABSOLUTELY NO LOYALTY

By: Elliott Lew Griffin

times I can be a real rouble rouser, but I don't know on this one, they got a little validity to what they are Saying. It's just bad that I got to report it.

All man, you know we are, California and this isn't Trump country, so they wanted Comey to give Trump hell, but all he did was run and tell. Then they are mad at what he ran and told about, claiming it was nothing to tell about. They thought that the head of the FBI guy was supposed to have a stiff upper lip, but the whole time his bottom lip has been quivering. Then when they found out that Comey's mouth was also running, they wanted to push Trump to the side and burn grass with Comey.

They claim he was supposed to be top secret, but the entire time he was the one who was doing all the squeaking. I don't know The American people are frustrated this whole Comey thing has gotten everyone irritated. I think it's cause Comey lied to them and said he was going to be the one to takedown Trump if the Russia collision thing didn't pan out, but now that the memos are released, they're mad at Comey's deceit. To say the least, the chatter is getting louder and the people are starting to talk. I've heard things like Comey has no backbone or worse he's spineless. They got a lack of trust in him and a lack of trust in everything. It's just all bad folks. I don't know why Comey just don't cancel his book tour. I'm going to be honest and tell you I don't know why he even started this book tour. Then a lot of people wanted to know why he wrote in his book about Trump's hand size and tan lines cause a lot of people thought that was kind of odd. And has since made them look at Comey in a whole new light.

JAMES COMEY

ABSOLUTELY NO LOYALTY

By: Elliott Lew Griffin

Then now with him cheerfully parading around town boasting and bragging about serial spewing classified information and that's not helping. Then to blame it on them for the reason he was doing it is definitely not helping the situation either folks. I don't know what we're going to do, but I know a lot of people will be glad when this Comey guy is locked up.

I don't know why he did that to Hillary and if that wasn't enough, he kept going. If anything after he did that to Hillary, he was supposed to go Incognito and now they say he is standing out like the only like black guy at the KKK rally or the only KKK at a black lives matter rally. I don't know folks, I'm just giving you the message as I'm getting them, I guess this is that serious and they want Comey to be prosecuted to the fullest extreme of the law. But it's like they said, Comey should be jailed.

I know we're waiting on some new information from Hannity but the more and more information I get on this Comey guy it's just getting worse. Hold on, let me see what they say right here? Comey was the head of the FBI and was supposed to be fearless, but yet we find out that he's actually a leaking fearful. The leader of the FBI is supposed to be commando, but the only commando Comey has been doing is running around underwear-less because he leaked into them too. All, that's all bad folks.

What they say, "get him pampers" (ALL)? "No, he definitely needs Huggies". All folks I don't know what to say, I'm breathless. I told you this was going topsy turvy from the beginning and you can't say that I didn't try to warn you. I know everyone's entitled to their opinion and I don't even know why I myself in the middle of this? I would think that Comey would be

195

JAMES COMEY

ABSOLUTELY NO LOYALTY

By: Elliott Lew Griffin

out there on this book tour trying to reestablish some type of integrity with the American people about the FBI, but I guess he just doesn't care because they fired him.

I know a lot of people are wondering why they even hired him. I just want to know why he can go around lying and boasting about leaking what they know is confidential information and he's not being prosecuted for it? Maybe we'll get that answer with Hannity when he comes on. I know Hannity is going to be screaming irate about it and but hopefully he can calm down and give us the answer? Your guess is as good as mine, but I'm going to try to find it out for you folks. And I hope that criminal referrals for Comey come soon because I honestly can't keep getting people's opinion on this.... This is a little too much for me, after I report the facts in this book I might have to put it in the ear plugs cause if the people don't buy this book , I'm not getting paid nothing to do this, if anything I'm losing time and money on this. And yes, Comey lies are killing me too, OMG make it stop already.

I'll tell you what I'm not a quitter, so I will continue to try to get to the bottom of this, but I will tell you this is starting to deteriorate really fast. I didn't know this Comey Guy was that bad. I didn't know this Comey Guy was that bad period.

I do know that Senator Chuck Grassley said: "Comey lied to him and Congress in the past", so I believe once they figure out the all the lies, they are going to arrest him. I will tell you like Sen. Grassley said and that was "just because you aren't hearing about the investigation on Comey don't worry we might not be hearing about it because all of this investigation is kept

JAMES COMEY

ABSOLUTELY NO LOYALTY

By: Elliott Lew Griffin

undercover". Apparently, he said it is like that because we got some good Patriots that are working on the investigation that don't leak information like Comey. All I can say is I hope he's right?

I know the American people are tired of all the corruption going on in our government and I know it's so bad that we can say that again, but I believe they are on it folks. Seriously, I believe they're in on it. I know a lot of stuff is kept under wraps so since the Comey investigation is so big, I can see them not telling us nothing about it. Someone talks on this one and I believe they will be in a cell next to Comey for their own leaking of top secret classified information. I even think this matter is being investigated by agencies outside the FBI, like the Department of Justice or even the U.S. Attorney's General's Office.

And a lot of people don't have much faith in Jeff Session either because he cracked under pressure when Congress started asking him questions. So, I don't know, but he was the one who had the nervous breakdown and just recused himself. I guess he couldn't handle no more questions folks, he couldn't handle no more questions?? So if you see him folks please don't ask him no more questions folks because we need him to focus on this Comey investigation and we can't afford for him to crack under pressure on this one. However, we now know Jeff Sessions has been gone for a while now and William Barr is our new Attorney General. That's why I say if you see Jeff Sessions don't even say nothing to him. As a matter of fact, please just don't even look at him, look the other way like you don't even see him and just let him go on with his life.

I honestly don't know how many questions they have asked him in Congress before he cracked under pressure, but at this point you're 1 maybe too many and honestly folks we're going to get Comey.

As far as Rod Rosenstein goes from what I gather the people don't really believe in him. I've been asking around that this is what they are questioning? They say an I quote: "If Rod Rosenstein is leading the Mueller investigation of Trump firing Comey for obstruction of justice and Rosenstein was the person that initially wrote Comey's termination letter, then how is Rosenstein in charge of the Mueller investigation that supposedly investigating whether Trump's firing of Comey amounted to obstruction of justice"?

I don't know that's the question the people want to know. To say the very least, I think their question has some legitimate truth to it, so the way they put it, someone is either cheating, or it's all a hoax folks. I'm reporting that something really doesn't sound right about it.

Then, hold onto your seatbelts cause there's more? I know we really can't take no more, but this may be a blockbuster to the whole investigation folks, so just bear with me please I'm trying to get you all the information. OK here we go, we got it ... Ah-ha! Are you sitting down or standing up? Well for some reason I knew this chapter was going to be topsy turvy so whatever you're doing you may want to be doing the opposite cause this piece of information may just have flipped the entire investigation on its head. I don't have concrete evidence but like I mentioned earlier there is no such law that's called collusion, so I know first-hand that you can't break a law that doesn't exist.

Then this is a new information that's coming in and it's from a 1972 statute that says that a sitting president "cannot" be indicted. I don't know I guess that's the law folks, so all of those that was hoping Trump would be indicted; the law in 1972 statute clearly says "No".

Apparently, this statue has further precedence during the Bill Clinton era when the people were trying to indict him for what he did. I'm looking at it right here and as I'm understanding it, I would say it's true... A sitting president cannot be indicted.

I think that's why they are trying to go for perjury? I will say that if Trump has to sit down with Miller or is forced to testify in front of Congress and he tells the truth whatever that may be then I'm either glad or sad to tell you which either side of the aisle you're on that he will not be charged with perjury. No matter what the truth is really?

Therefore, my sources are saying that the entire rumor that Trump would or even could be indicted is all just another hoax folks. I don't know. They created the law, so they know the law, unless I'm not reading this right. I don't know why they are lying to yawl. Either way if you're happy or sad, we are still going to get James Comey, Andrew McCabe, and a few others out of this. So, on that note we're going to take a quick break folks, so just bear with me as I'm trying to get you all the information I can and please keep reading ...

JAMES COMEY – ABSOLUTELY NO LOYALTY

COMEY

YOU'RE GOING TO JAIL IN THE END!!!

CHAPTER 15

JAMES COMEY

A DIRTY ROTTEN SCOUNDREL!

I don't even know why he got all of this started. This dude is like rain on your wedding day. Just look at the bright side... At least you got married. Somebody Loves You. Like I always say I got to start writing love stories. I think I can write a great love story. (Like I love you baby...) So, you know I called him a dirty rotten scoundrel cause there's more right?

This dude is all bad folks, he's just all bad period. Well apparently on this worldwide book tour Comey admitted that part of the Russian Steel Dossier that he presented to the judge to be permitted to spy on the Trump campaign with unreliable. So not only did he not tell the judge that it was paid for in part by the DNC and the Hillary Clinton campaign, but apparently he knew according to his own words that it was really unreliable before he submitted it to the judges.

JAMES COMEY

ABSOLUTELY NO LOYALTY

By: Elliott Lew Griffin

Yeah, this guy isn't smart at all. (There went my chances of selling books), I don't think nobody would want to read all of this. This might really be too bad of a read for them. If you're reading this don't tell them all these folks. Just keep it a secret. We're going to close this chapter... Please don't tell anybody I'm sorry and please keep reading...Your reading...

JAMES COMEY – ABSOLUTELY NO LOYALTY

HONESTLY, WHAT CAN I REALLY SAY

JAMES COMEY

A REAL NIGHTMARE ON ELM STREET

FOLKS!

CHAPTER 16

JAMES COMEY
A HIGHER LOYALTY?
I THINK NOT!!!!

You know what, as a matter of fact I know not folks .... That's not even a question. This Comey guy is that bad period. They are saying he's an embarrassment to the FBI Bureau so much that he would make J. Edgar Hoover turn over in his grave. Don't worry folks, I'm hearing new reports that he turned back over to his rightful resting position after he heard about our worst FBI Deputy Director in United States History...Lacking Candor McCabe!

I don't know, apparently that's what they are calling Andrew McCabe now.... This is turning into an old western film type of name thing now. I guess it's "Slippery Shady James Comey" and "Lacking Candor McCabe". The two worst guys in FBI history

JAMES COMEY

ABSOLUTELY NO LOYALTY

By: Elliott Lew Griffin

period. Don't worry folks this is not an old western film and we're going to prosecute them.

I'll tell you what would make a good one, Slippery Slopey James Comey and Lacking Candor Andrew McCabe strikes again. They say Slippery Shady James Comey can slip his way through anything and Lacking Candor McCabe can lie his way through anything. I don't know folks we're going to get them; we are going to get them.

You know what, I was trying to go into a fiction type of thing because I'm pretty sure you don't want to hear the truth about what I'm going to tell you and the latest developments in the Comey case, it's not good folks, it's not good at all.

These two have just done so much that it's almost depressing to have discovered it all. Maybe that's how they get away with it all? They just do so much that it's overwhelming to the point that it makes you just want to give up. Like man you win. I give up...whatever? These two are the worst dynamic dual to ever have such a high-ranking mainstream scandal. The crazy part about it is they would have to both be from the same Bureau and they would both have to be one and two. That's what's getting people the most is how they were able to get away with it for so long and that's because they were both the head guys in charge.

I tell you one thing folks, I think Hannity and I got it all for you right here. Like Hannity has been predicting for quite some time and that 2018 is going to be the year of the boomerang. His secret plan to get Trump's investigated has worked but in investigating Trump they have discovered that both he and

JAMES COMEY

ABSOLUTELY NO LOYALTY

By: Elliott Lew Griffin

Lacking Candor McCabe have been involved in the biggest abuse of power corruption scandals in US history.

The whole time Comey thought he was going to get back at trump for firing him, but the entire investigation has turned around on him and headed back in his direction at speeds he can't even imagine. I bet you he's thinking why did he do this? They say he's going to finish his book tour because to stop midstream would look a little guilty. I think this is what's going to cost him. He did the CNN Town Hall meeting interview with Anderson Cooper and was hoping for a hero's welcome but was met with some tough questions that he really didn't have answers for.

I also looked into 28 U.S.C. section 1001 and I found out that's a charge of lying to federal investigators. They say Comey is on the hook for that one as well because he's been lying to Congress who been investigating him since the beginning. One of the biggest developments in Comey's case is the fact that he's now admitted to stealing the confidential documents from the FBI building and leaking them to three separate people. At first, he kept claiming it was one and now we know through his new admission that there was a total of three.

The crazy part is that the three people that Comey leaked the top secret FBI documents to were all attorneys and now with the money he just received from his book deal he went and hired him at least two of them to represent him in this matter. They are saying he hired them to invoke the attorney client privileges, but some of my other source are saying that Comey may have handed them an over the table pay off - so they don't tell. I'll tell

JAMES COMEY

ABSOLUTELY NO LOYALTY

By: Elliott Lew Griffin

you what, they are saying that the hiring of the two attorneys that he leaked the top secret documents to are looking very suspicious and many of the people want to know more about it. All I know is my sources are claiming that Comey took seven memos from the FBI's buildings and four of them had top secret classified information on them. However, he is claiming that he did not leave the four top secret classified documents with these attorneys so they are alleging that Comey may have hired these attorneys that he leaked the classified documents to just so they would say he did not leave the classified documents to them. But how else did they get them right?

I don't know folks it's all looking funny. They say he's either trying to buy his way out of it, or these attorneys are blackmailing him. They are reporting that this could be a strong possibility that it may be blackmail because let's face it, they know beyond a reasonable doubt Comey messed up and should be prosecuted for it.

Don't get me wrong, but this is the theory they are saying and that is if Comey did not pay these attorney's fees they wanted today and not now, but right now. Then I'm pretty they were still going to leak our top secret classified information to them. I'm going to be honest folks, and even quote James Comey on this one "it's possible".

I don't know how much he's paying them to keep quiet or how much they are blackmailing him for, but my sources are under the impression that it's either hush money or blackmail money that he's paying these attorneys for.

JAMES COMEY

ABSOLUTELY NO LOYALTY

By: Elliott Lew Griffin

After I found out Comey was either paying his attorneys hush money or being blackmailed, I talked to another source who claimed that Congress went about shelling out the memos to the press all along. They assert that while they leaked highly classified information to the press that no one should have been privileged to see until the investigation is over. In short, they messed up too. Apparently, they let the all-time ousting of James Comey get the better half of their overall judgment in an attempt to discredit Comey in wake of his book tour. However, this information should not have been release to the public until the initial investigation was over.

It's going down folks it's going down. The Republican Congress was in the rush to clear Trump and my sources claim they should have been more focused on the leaking of these men to the two separate attorneys that Comey leaked the memos too. They contend that before they released these memos to the public that they should have raided these two attorneys' offices to see what memos they were in possession of. If they were in possession of all the memos before they were released, then that would have indicated that Comey leaked all of the memos to them and their company was further lying the whole time.

They're saying and I don't know if I should be telling you this, but they claimed that since Congress did redact some of the memos before they released them, that confirms they had confidential information on them. Now my sources are saying they may still raid these attorney's offices like they raided Michael Cohen's office to see if he was in possession of the non-redacted memos which was still indicate that Comey leak them to them.

Your guess is as good as mine on what they're going to do, but they are claiming that the Republican Congress may have also violated rules and regulations of releasing confidential information of an ongoing information too. To say the least, everything is just going all bad.

According to the rules of the FBI and DOJ, no information whatsoever is to be released until the investigation is over and the Republican Congress members violated that rule when releasing these memos to the public because they were still the subject of an ongoing criminal investigation of obstructing of justice against Trump. My sources are saying that the DOJ and Attorney General's Office should investigate why Congress would release documents to the public that were the primary source of an investigation against the U.S. President. From what I hear this is not too much different than what they are partially blaming Comey for doing in the Hillary Clinton investigation. That was, he was not to give out or indulge any information on an ongoing subject of a criminal investigation and yet Congress has done the same damn thing, so I don't know what the ramifications are ,or what the outcome will be or would be for their actions, but somebody may have to answer for that since the release of this information violated the protocol because the investigation against Trump had not been concluded yet.

We're going to see folks; we're going to see. All of this kind of makes sense to me, it's kind of makes sense to me. I also know that they're still waiting on the communications between James

JAMES COMEY

ABSOLUTELY NO LOYALTY

By: Elliott Lew Griffin

Comey and Robert Mueller and they want that communication information before they question Comey again on Capitol Hill. They want to know what he said to Mueller already so when they questioned him again, he won't be able to continue to play both sides and lie to everyone in the middle.

I'll tell you what, just in the last month since Comey started his book tour everything then boomeranged on him and it's got him backpedaling already. Hiring two attorneys that he's leaked the memo too was an indication that he's trying to cover his tracks or like my sources say, they seen Comey recently acquire a mass amount of wealth from his book deal and are blackmailing him for piece of it. How much is a piece, stay tuned we will try to find that out for you folks...you know how we do it?

Like I say if there is some information that you're confused about or want to know more about the Comey investigation I'm going to tell you to log on Hannity.com and he should have the latest developments on the Comey investigation on there. We're going to get to the bottom of this folks. With that said, please stay tuned and keep reading...

JAMES COMEY – ABSOLUTELY NO LOYALTY

REP. TREY GOWDY:

"WHAT COMEY CALLS A "LEAK"

...

THE REST OF US CALL A FELONY"

CHAPTER 17

JAMES COMEY
A REPUBLICAN!

All folks...I don't know what to tell you? The stories are just so conflicting now that I'm having a hard time trying to keep them straight. So, if I seem to be conflicted at any time, don't think it's me folks, it's them. They don't know if they're hanging are washing, just like that Comey guy doesn't know if he's a Democrat or Republican, we just want to get the truth out of him. Apparently after the latest round of interviews he's not a Republican and he hasn't been a Republican since 2012, but they have evidence that his voter registration proves otherwise. Yeah come on Comey, just quit lying.

My personal sources are saying that he's just doing this to appease the Democrats that's buying his book cause he even wrote in there that the country would be better ran with Hillary than with Trump and everyone knows the Democrats love to hear that. However, that same source is marveling at how well Comey has been able to play the Democrats especially since she believes that Comey is only doing this as an alibi to cover his

JAMES COMEY

ABSOLUTELY NO LOYALTY

By: Elliott Lew Griffin

tracks for meddling in the 2016 presidential election and that's Hillary Clinton party folks. She claims this is the perfect cover for anyone looking to get away with violating federal election laws which many have said Comey violated when breaking FBI protocol.

However, Comey has turned to the Democrats for solace. It is rumored that the Republican said that the Democrats could keep Comey because they don't want him on their side because he's a liar, a leaker, and a weasel. I don't know how high that goes in the ranking officials of the Republican officials but that is a clear message from Trump campaign that James Comey is no longer welcome in the Republican Party and if his meddling in the 2016 presidential election did help Hillary lose and get Trump elected then...thank you, they're alleging.

I don't know folks; you can't make this stuff up. I am also getting some reports that the Republicans may take it to the voters that Democrats are harvesting liar leakers like James Comey that should otherwise be prosecuted. Reports here are they are going to claim during the 2018 midterms that if the Democrats are again the majority in the house that they will let Comey off the hook for his crimes. I mean can a Democrat majority run House help Comey get off and then why would they want to? I don't know, something's not adding up folks cause if anything I would think that the Democrats would want to prosecute James Comey for meddling in the 2016 election? All I would say is your guess is as good as mine because it's appearing like the facts change every day and we can't get the truth out of anybody.

JAMES COMEY

ABSOLUTELY NO LOYALTY

By: Elliott Lew Griffin

I'll tell you what, we're just going to stick with Hannity folks. Everything he has been saying for the past year about Comey is starting to come full circle. That's why I said 2018 will be the year of the boomerang because he had the inside scoop and knew the facts the entire time. The Russian hoax, yeah was a Russian hoax. And spent mins going down that fox hole and for what...a hoax. He said that the entire time, you all know that folks. I know he takes a lot of backlash for not being part of the hate Trump media that many news networks appear to be coming, but I really like Hannity for two reasons, one, you always get the inside scoop on all the corruption that's going on inside our governmental institutions and two, you always get what's good going on in our country too.

What they say every day is just not doom and gloom all the time folks like the Democrats want to make it appear. Just like the other day he was talking about how 14 states hit record low unemployment in the United States history. That is a fact that I'm proud of as a Patriot to see that my fellow countrymen and countrywomen have jobs to support their families. Black and Hispanic unemployment is at an incredibly low level across our nation, so that is seriously something to be proud about. Then like Hannity has said that the left is looking a little defaced about that and it's true. At times they have shown that they would rather see our country fail, then to give an ounce of credit to Donald Trump and to me it's just not right. At some point they have to quit caring about who gets the credit and or learn to give credit when credit is due and move on period. Now they're saying that the Republicans did that to the Democrats when the Democrats were in office, so now we're just seeing the flip side

215

of the coin, but I don't think the hatred has ever been this bad. The dividing of this presidential cycle is extreme. Polar opposites and there are no in-between. I tell you what, people ask me all the time which side I'm on and I'm gladly tell them that I'm on the American people side. That is whatever is best for the Country. I don't do sides when the country is involved.

Like I said, whichever side is right for the American people at the time I'm rolling with them. To me I'm in it for the good of the people and not for which side is which. Just the other day someone asked me if I was independent of all parties and you know what I told them, "NO", I am the sum of all parties. He laughed when I told him that I was an Independent Democratic Republican that likes to drink green tea. Ha-ha. He thought that was a good one. I laughed and walked away I knew it was one too. Then he asked me if I was interested in socialism or capitalism, I gladly told him that I was into idealism because a great idea is going to get you to your destination every time. Why am I sharing this with you because I'm trying to broaden your horizon folks?

Like they say, you vote Republican and you get Republican ideas. You vote Democrat and you get Democrat ideas. I don't know folks, I'm just in it for the best American ideas. You see I wrote the book on James Comey Absolutely No Loyalty and that's because I'm really into it for the idea. Like hey, that sounds like an Amazing idea, then let's do it. I don't know folks, I'm just trying, so please bear with me and please keep reading ...

JAMES COMEY - ABSOLUTELY NO LOYALTY

I NEVER GIVE THEM HELL
I JUST TELL THE TRUTH...
AND THEY THINK ITS HELL
-HARRY S. TRUMAN

CHAPTER 18

JAMES COMEY
PAYING OUT HUSH MONEY FOLKS

The people I talk to say it's official, James Comey is paying out hush money to the attorneys he leaked the memos too. He's trying to lock them into an attorney client privilege contract, but don't worry folks, it's not going to work. He's already admitted to taking them without consent and leaking them, so there's no getting around it, he will go to jail. And or he should go to jail, right?

I'll tell you what, I would have thought that as Comey book tour and interviews went on that his explanations would have gotten better, but his answers have only gotten worse. To say the least, his book tour has gone down in a tailspin and have kicked up more dust than a whirl wind. It has taken America by surprise and has completely sent whatever face Comey had left right into a nosedive. It's like he jumped from the highest ranking official in the FBI and plummeted straight into the ground. A cold and

JAMES COMEY

ABSOLUTELY NO LOYALTY

By: Elliott Lew Griffin

damp prison cell. If his career isn't over yet, it's over now. Good thing he said in his latest interview that he wasn't going to run for any government office, we dodged a bullet on that one. James Comey in another governmental position, we would deserve everything we had coming if we allowed that to happen again. This guy is all bad and even if the media isn't tired of hearing about him already, I am. So actually, I'm even surprised you bought the book, thank you, I really appreciate that for real. I know writing about James Comey and company I'm probably going down with the worst book in United States history. No sells, but my own. Like, I guess that's what I get when deciding to write about the worse FBI director in the United States history. I honestly don't know what I was thinking, it was the cover that got me? You too? Well I guess that's why they always said don't choose a book by its cover, because if I weren't so far into this, I would probably scrap this idea already. Why? Because everybody already knows James Comey has Absolutely No Loyalty.

Like, what was I thinking, I don't want to say that I suckered you into buying it by saying it was (A MUST READ) but come on...a book about Slippery Slopey James Comey, sorry, but that's a no read. I was just hoping the title of the book would hook you. And again, thank you for buying it. We are going to try to do the best we can with the rest of what we have, but with Comey you already know, he's all bad folks. What more can I say... You want to hear something good about him? I'm sorry to tell you there is none!!!

JAMES COMEY

ABSOLUTELY NO LOYALTY

By: Elliott Lew Griffin

I will tell you that in Comey's recent sit-down interview with Fox News, he still claimed not to know that the Steele dossier was Funded by the DNC and the Hillary Clinton campaign. However? Like the guy came right on after him and said Comey's lied and lied and lied, so that should tell you something folks, he lied and lied and lied.

Oh, he even came up with another excuse in his card or should I say bag of tricks when he started saying: To My Recollection. Well at least we all know that Comey's recollection or memory isn't too good. I would even hate to say that he's distorted facts because in actuality he's ripped them apart. What can I say, he's James Comey right, the worst FBI Director in all of United States history? Like who was the FBI director that was running the show in 2016 – 2017? Yeah folks, history should stop reporting on bad people for fear that history would be repeated. I guess that's how we ran into the number two guy Lacking Candor Andrew McCabe, he was trying to get his place in history cemented as well and to say the least it's definitely set in stone that he's going down as the second worse FBI guy in US history.

I'll tell you what, we are living in the times of the biggest corrupt governmental scandals in US history. I don't even know how all of these people have been able to get away with it for so long. All I can say is I'm glad that it's finally starting to surface. The crazy part is they were the ones that opened this investigation on Trump and now it's backfired on them. The boomerang is coming, so don't try to run now Comey. It's all too late, we're going to get you Comey! For real, everyone's mad at him. He might have bit off a little more than he could chew on

JAMES COMEY

ABSOLUTELY NO LOYALTY

By: Elliott Lew Griffin

this one. I know I might exaggerate sometimes but like Kahlil Gibran has said: "Exaggeration is just the truth that lost his temper".

However, with Comey I didn't even lose my temper, he really did all of this I'm telling you. I know it may seem like an exaggeration, but come on where talking about Slippery Shady James Comey here, so everything we say I'm pretty sure is still an understatement. The crazy part is, he's trying to claim that all of the errors or mistakes, but not only were they all blunders, they were complete epic failures. Like they say, where there's smoke there's fire and right now we are seeing the smoke, but the Comey fire is worse than what we ever thought possible or imaginable.

Like I say, wildfires burns forests and destroys homes, but all the lying to the people and the if I say judges Comey has done has completely burned down our democracy and destroyed lives. Trust and believe these dudes didn't just start lying today. I guarantee you they have a long history and a consistent pattern dating back decades.

We're just now seeing the aftermath, or the domino effect of it cause they just got caught, but if we were to really start digging into their past, I'm willing to bet it goes all the way back to the very beginning. I mean look at Comey now after all of these years as a federal prosecutor and as the FBI Director and he can't even answer a truthful question today.... So, what do you think he was doing way back in the day? (Yeah, I don't even want to know myself)? For real, I mean look how callous and corrupt these people can be. Then we look at the fact that he was once a federal prosecutor and see that he definitely cheated people somehow and probably in every way.

Not only did he withhold key evidence from the FISA Judge about the Hillary Clinton and the DNC paid for Russian dossier , but he still lying to us the American people to this day that he don't know if they were the ones that paid for it, or not. I would say that this guy is confused but Comey told one too many fabricated stories for us to not find that it's all a lie. His story has changed too many times and I don't know about you, but I'm glad I didn't read his book because I would have found at least four different ways on how he misrepresented his story. What can I say folks, I'm an expert liar finder? Like, that didn't add up, or that it makes sense and you know what attracted me to Comey the most was the title of his book A Higher Loyalty. When I see that I instantly thought WHAT? YEAH RIGHT? JAMES COMEY - ABSOLUTELY NO LOYALTY.

I'm serious, had he titled it anything other than that, I know I and many people wouldn't have even made a fuss about it, but the fact that he titled it that... is what created all of this madness. Like when I saw the cover of his book it just hit me like a ton of bricks and to be honest it was just dispiriting to me as American Patriot to see him use that as his book title. Like not on my watch, for real .... I don't know who he thinks he is, but he's not going to get away with its folks, not on my watch. How about yours?

When I get done with him he's going to be stained, black eyed, dishonored, bad named and a low down dirty shame, but then again he doesn't need me to do that... he's done a pretty good job of doing that to himself. I'm just laying out some of the truth

JAMES COMEY

ABSOLUTELY NO LOYALTY

By: Elliott Lew Griffin

here. His name is mud and to say the very least, he did it to himself.

I know it's one thing for him to incur disgrace upon his own face, but don't make a mockery out of the country I love in doing so. That's when I have a problem. Like what did he just say? He did all of his corruption for A Higher Loyalty to us the American people, like how sadistic that is ??? Don't worry folks, we are going to lay into him the real old school Apple pie and Chevrolet American way and beat him into submission. I know the Buck stops here and hey he sowed it, so now he's going to reap it. All Comey had to do was tell us he wanted to go to jail, he didn't have to commit treason by leaking our top-secret government documents in order to do so. To be honest, I guess it was the money he was after and he got it with his book deal, but it's too bad he's going to have to spend it all on his legal defense team in attempt to keep his butt out of jail. Then he's still going.

I wouldn't be surprised to see him plead guilty once he's charged because really, he's only going to get a couple of years. He'll do about 18 months off of that and be released. Probably with the release of another book titled I'm rehabilitated or again his new book Saving Justice, but yeah right? Like I said James Comey Murdered Justice.

He could even dummy it down and call it A Higher Royalty until the truth and plot unfolds because people are always interested in that. The crazy part is if we had to go through all of this just to get him locked in a cell for months, and or worse probation, did we really win in the end?

We the people will have to pay hundreds of thousands to prosecute him for a highly publicized trial and appeal. Then even

JAMES COMEY

ABSOLUTELY NO LOYALTY

By: Elliott Lew Griffin

after we get him in a cell we're going to have to pay another couple hundred grand for him to stay there, so we're really talking about 3 to 400 grand to prosecute Comey and he's only going to get about 18 months in jail for all of his crimes. Maybe even probation? While I guess it's like they've always said: there is no price on justice folks, there is no price on justice.

And since he's making a mockery out of us the American People as to why he did it, then your darn right we want to prosecute him for it. Him blaming his felonious reasons on us is the straw that broke the camel's back and for that we want our day in court. We have been looking for an end all solution in our government for a very long time and people like James Comey has been our problem this entire time. So now not only do we want to prosecute him for retribution, but we must prosecute him to send a clear message that this type of behavior will no longer be tolerated in our government officials.

Anyhow folk's, we are still at the tip of the iceberg and to be honest I don't think we're going to make it to the bottom, he just did too much, but any event please keep reading...

JAMES COMEY - ABSOLUTELY NO LOYALTY

I'M GLAD TRUMP FIRED JAMES COMEY

CHAPTER 19

JAMES COMEY
A MAD DISGRUNTLED
EMPLOYEE

I'll tell you what, this Comey guy is just a little bit of everything. No wonder why he's been all over the news, he then did everything in the book. I know I keep saying this guy is all bad folks, but how much more do you want to hear and or how much more can you possibly take. This book then went from bad to just plain helter skelter and you're still here wanting to hear more, I love it.... Well you better grab a Scooby snack because there's more. For real, that's who we need on this Comey trail is Scobey-doo. I bet you he can get to the bottom of this.

Well folks, we officially have a crossfire between Slippery Shady James Comey and Lacking Candor Andrew McCabe, but which one to believe... Your guess is just as good as mine. Hey, being that these guys are both the worst guys in FBI history, or at least in today's role of FBI history, all I can say is they're a 50/50 chance they're lying or is it just 100/100 percent chance they're both lying . Where there is new information out there that Lacking Candor McCabe is saying that Slippery Shady James

JAMES COMEY

ABSOLUTELY NO LOYALTY

By: Elliott Lew Griffin

Comey was authorizing all the leaking, but they're saying that the world must be cautious of that information because it is coming from none other than Lacking Candor Andrew McCabe?

Then, this is what I say, if Comey was authorizing all of the leaks when he was in charge, who was authorizing all of the leaks when McCabe was in charge? Maybe he never got the memo that Comey was fired before he was, or do you think Comey was still ordering him to leak the information after he was fired. I don't know good folks, I told you all of this just went to helter skelter. I thought you would have gotten a hint when I said that. All I know is that everybody is telling on everybody and don't nobody know who to believe because their all proven liars. What do you do, take the word of the one that lied the least? Or the one that lied the most?? Or do you just not believe either one of them.

We're trying to figure it out folks, but if we were to do a public study of whose word do you take as credible Slippers Shady James Comey or Lacking Candor Andrew McCabe? Stay tuned folks, all I can say is please keep reading...

JAMES COMEY - ABSOLUTELY NO LOYALTY

AREN'T YOU GLAD TRUMP FIRED COMEY TOO??

JAMES COMEY

ABSOLUTELY NO LOYALTY

By: Elliott Lew Griffin

THE WORST FBI DIRECTOR IN UNITED STATES HISTORY

CHAPTER 20

JAMES COMEY ABUSED HIS POWER

They say that James Comey had one of the biggest abuses of power scandals in United States history when he used his power as FBI director to interfere with the 2016 presidential election. I mean this doesn't delegitimize Trump as the president because he won fair and square. I think almost everyone knew that Hillary Clinton was crooked for deleting her 33,000 emails during that investigation, so when the people went to the polls, they knew about that information already, but Comey didn't help the cause when he threw in a monkey wrench in the matter and should be imprisoned for doing so.

Without a doubt Comey usurped our democracy with his antics and since he broke all FBI protocol when doing so clearly proves that he had no reasonable explanation for his actions. That's why my report says here that he should be tried for violating federal election laws and because he violated FBI protocol in doing so, my sources say that is enough to get a conviction. They say it doesn't matter whether his actions actually swayed the election either way, but it's based on the fact that he tried.

JAMES COMEY

ABSOLUTELY NO LOYALTY

By: Elliott Lew Griffin

If you're not too familiar with the facts of this case, in connection with a federal investigation case against Anthony Weiner, the strange ex-husband of Hillary Clinton's right hand gal Houma, The FBI agents searched Wieners computer and discovered emails on there between Huma and Hillary. At that time, the FBI didn't know if those emails were duplicates of the ones already reviewed, or if they were personal or work related. And to say the least, James Comey absolutely knew nothing about them.

Yet, two days before Comey received a warrant to look at the emails, Comey had already sent a letter to 8 different congressional committees saying the FBI has learned of the existence of emails that appear to be pertinent to the Hillary Clinton's closed email investigation. Although Comey's letter did further state the FBI cannot access whether or not this material may be significant, it was all but too late as Jason Chaffetz, the then chairman of the House Oversight Committee had already tweeted out case reopened.

With a public statement like this, Chavez had to have known that even a unverified tweet like this was politically devastating to the Hillary Clinton campaign. The most bizarre part is before he even knew the facts of these new emails, he had taken steps to interfere with the 2016 presidential election.

Comey's actions were swiftly condemned by the Justice Department Officials and the Department of Justice Inspector General also opened an investigation into Comey's conduct. A lot of people thought that the Inspector General was going to find that Comey violated federal election laws because Comey violated the FBI's longstanding policy of not confirming or

JAMES COMEY

ABSOLUTELY NO LOYALTY

By: Elliott Lew Griffin

denying the existence of an investigation when reopening the Hillary Clinton email investigation so close to the election.

Now the crazy part is, before Comey sent the letter to the Justice Department officials, they had already reminded Comey and his deputies of the longstanding policy to avoid any activities that could be viewed as influencing the election. Also, in the same letter the Justice Department officials had told Comey that there was no need to inform Congress about the Hillary emails until the FBI had determined if they were pertinent to the investigation, but Comey violated that order as well.

The part that gets me the most is that Comey recently admitted in his interview with George Stephanopoulos that a member of his FBI team told him that his actions of reopening this investigation so close to the election would sway voters the other way and Comey still did it...without ever reviewing any of the new emails. Comey also claimed in this same interview that he did so because it was a case of intense public interest. However, as Matt Miller, the Justice Department's Public Affairs officer pointed out that the Department investigates cases involving extreme public interests all the time, and therefore that was no reason for Comey to violate the FBI's long-standing judicial policy.

I will note that his October 28th, 2016 letter reopening the Hillary Clinton email investigation did lead to a week of wall to wall negative coverage of the Hillary Clinton campaign. A look at the nation's top five newspapers found that together they published 100 stories mentioning the email controversy in the days after Comey's letter, nearly half on the front page, but then

JAMES COMEY

ABSOLUTELY NO LOYALTY

By: Elliott Lew Griffin

Hillary's email investigation was a hot topic leading up to the election and it was one of the lead stories in the nation new cycle that election year as well. It is also how she got the name AKA crooked Hillary. And hey she's the one that deleted the 33,000 emails not me for sure right, so she needs to come to terms and face the facts of what SHE DID and to be honest, I believe she did that already when she did not run for the 2020 presidential election. She knew she was Crooked Hillary and she couldn't overcome it. Why? Because she's Crooked Hillary and there's no escaping that. That's the entire reason why she didn't run in 2020 presidential election. I'm sorry that's Hillary Clinton but I doubt that she would ever give up on the presidency unless she knew that she couldn't win. And we all know the name alone "Crooked Hillary" was the real reason she would never run again. What can I say, but Trump branded her for life? Crooked Hillary sold like no other.

However back to Comey.... To me the weird part was that on Sunday afternoon, a weekend and 36 hours before Election Day Comey sent another letter explaining that, in fact there was no evidence to change his conclusion from July of 2016. Of course, the rest is history and Donald Trump won.

In any event, he should still be investigated for his actions especially since this wasn't the first time, he did this. Early in July of 2016, he came out criticizing Hillary in a press conference that he also broke FBI protocol on. So if once was enough, he continuously broke the rule of law during our 2016 presidential cycle.

On May 19th, Rod Rosenstein testified before Congress that Comey's July press conference was profoundly wrong and unfair.

JAMES COMEY

ABSOLUTELY NO LOYALTY

By: Elliott Lew Griffin

Then according to Rosenstein's July 5th, 2017 press conference, Rosenstein stated that Comey usurped the Attorney Generals authority, violated deeply ingrained rules and traditions of the Justice Department and ignored another longstanding principle "we do not hold press conferences to release the derogatory information about the subject of a declined criminal investigation".

As Matt Miller further stated that "Comey's willingness to reprimand publicly a figure against whom he believes there is no basis for criminal charges should trouble anyone who believes in the rule of law and fundamental principles of fairness".

I don't know folks, it's definitely troubling to me because I believe in the fundamental principles of our laws and Comey just broke almost every single one of them. I mean we have literally condemned the Russians for meddling in our election, but here we have allowed the meddling of James Comey to go unpunished. I know there are a lot of investigations going on, but I believe that this is of the most seriousness and we should hold Comey's feet to the flames, especially since he now has admitted to doing so after he looked at the polls. This to me shows intent and maybe he didn't do it to elect Donald Trump, but he definitely did it in disgorge to Hillary Clinton. Like I say again, James Comey himself said that he didn't start the investigation on Hillary Clinton until after he looked at the polls and must have saw her winning. Why? Because the polls showed Hillary was winning. And again, showing his intent on meddling in the 2016 presidential election.

Then not to mention, in that same token, Comey revealed the Hillary information and concealed the Trump information. I'll

JAMES COMEY

ABSOLUTELY NO LOYALTY

By: Elliott Lew Griffin

tell you what, all of fits right into the James Comey character that we have to come to find out and that's James Comey does liar, leaky, sneaky, weasel move and we should hold James Comey accountable for his corrupts actions right? Like he said, "I don't do lying sneaky leaky weasel moves", yet we find out that he do lying leaky sneaky weasel moves. That's James Comey folks a lying leaky sneaky weasel.

I will say this, the more the American people pay Comey for his book, the further we praise this type of criminal behavior. Like I said, I'm surprised his book has sold so well given the fact that he is hated by both sides. I bet you Hillary Clinton is hating it and Donald Trump has been loving the way, he has shown a willingness to flat out lie to the public like this. To say the least, it has been an interesting story to watch unfold. It definitely threw me for a loop, or two.

It seemed like every time Comey opened his mouth, he's said something else. I guess it comes as no surprise that I had to loop back around to my notes just to make sure I was writing it down right; yeah, he said the opposite. In all just, I found that it was easier to write what he said and then right below it write the opposite, so that way I no longer had to loop back around and write the opposite when he said the opposite. What a loser... James Comey a real loser.

I'm telling you, reporting on James Comey was a lot harder than it looked. I was already confused by what I know he did versus what he said in his interview's that I'm kind of thankful I didn't read his book. If I had to report on a third or fourth interpretation of what he said, I would have just gave up. I'm not even going to ******** you folks. I would have just thrown my

235

JAMES COMEY

ABSOLUTELY NO LOYALTY

By: Elliott Lew Griffin

hands in the air and said you know what this guy is officially a scumbag. Like this guy has so many lies that I can't even keep them straight and that's all Bad. No wonder why he couldn't keep track of what he said, he has so many different versions of the story, that I'm having trouble keeping up with them and I'm the one writing the story. Like, this is definitely above my pay grade. I know if I had to read his book just for fun I would have been lost. Like on page 5 he said? Page 10 was the opposite and Page 20 was an entirely different story. I know by page 40 that story would have metastasize into four other stories and heaven forbid by page 80 I would have thought I was reading 8 unidentical stories with so many different variables, that if I had to write a book after that, I would have just wrote 3 words that said: Yeah, He Lied. But I will tell you what 3 words we should all be screaming and that is "lock him up"... "lock him up"... "lock him up" "lock him up" that's what we should all be screaming because he just screwed us so bad that it's not even entertaining to listen to anymore, or watch, if it ever was. I tell you I've been having a hard time writing this book about him and I'm hardly the one to be at a loss for words or imagination, but messing with this guy, he just takes the cake every time. I see why they haven't prosecuted him yet; he just makes you want to give up. Like I had enough. We don't want to hear nothing else about him. If his interviews haven't went on long enough and to be honest, I just quit watching them. Like what am I going to watch that for? I don't feel like being lied to today and or hearing another lame excuse about why he did it and I know I can't take another story about how he didn't know.

JAMES COMEY

ABSOLUTELY NO LOYALTY

By: Elliott Lew Griffin

Like make it stop already please. Don't worry folks, you're almost to the end, I can feel it coming. I know if you're not tired of reading about Comey, then I'm tired of writing about him. Somebody's going to give, and I was hoping it was me before you because I know if it was you before me, then you might not be buying another book for me. Hey what can I say but that's true right.

I wonder how do you write a good book about a bad person? Like do people go in reading about a bad person expecting to read a good book. I don't know, either way I did the best I could folks. Really, I only asked that because I heard Matt Damion talking about making a movie on Harvey Weinstein and I thought that has to be one of the worst movies ever. Like who's going to go watch that unless they're going to hang him in the end or something. I mean he's goanna get the electric chair in the end or something. I mean people may want to watch that, but to just sit there and watch how Harvey Weinstein abused women I'm sorry to tell you but I don't think I will be watching that no time soon. However, or whomever do go watching that movie, at least we know who to keep our eyes on because they are into some sadistic stuff right. Then like I say I don't know why it took so long to lock Harvey Weinstein up. I thought his trial would have been held in the courtroom right next door to Bill Cosby and convicted on the same day. Man, we got to lock up so many people it's pathetic. For real, we got to start screaming lock these corrupt people up.

However since this book was written so long ago we all know that Harvey Weinstein is now locked up and that he will probably be locked up for a very very very very very long time, but again since I wrote this book so long ago it's a little outdated, so bear with me please folks you already know your reading... James Comey Absolutely No Loyalty.

But then like I talk about, how these people are still on the streets #WOW. If the average Joe blow did all of this, they would be underneath the jail, but since Comey did it and got an amazing book deal and now they're making a movie of Harvey Weinstein? I'm sorry to say this type of behavior should not be glorified in no way shape or form. Then I could see if he was going to do decades behind bars like what Bill Cosby is looking at but to do a movie about his life is sending the wrong message to the rest of the world. It's like saying woman abuse is OK. Like I say, maybe they burn him at the stake in the end, like that scumbag.... I don't know folks, if I did write a book on Harvey Weinstein, it would definitely begin and end with we got that bastard folks. For real, have all kinds of women out there kicking on him. He's in for a world of trouble and he better hope the officer that shows up isn't a woman too. Just talking about making a movie about Harvey Weinstein, women are going to be out there picketing and the sick thing about it all, is Harvey Weinstein is probably behind the whole damn thing? Hit them with James Comey "it's possible".

Actually, I hope someone do write the Harvey Weinstein book, then that means my James comedy book won't go down as the worst book in history. I know I can't afford to write a book about Harvey Weinstein, that would mean I would have the two worst books in United States history. Don't worry folks, you're not reading Harvey Weinstein right now, but they really need to lock that dude up too. What he did and got away with, should never be permissible without jail, that's for sure. Anyhow again I'm sorry about the minor Weinstein interruption folks because again we all know that Harvey Weinstein is locked up. Harvey Weinstein is locked up. So, without further ado I'm going to go back to our favorite program right and that is...

JAMES COMEY - ABSOLUTELY NO LOYALTY

LOCK
HARVEY WEINSTEIN UP TOO

OH
THEY DID ALREADY...

GOOD!

I KNOW I WROTE THIS BOOK A FEW YEARS BACK, BUT NEVER PUT IT OUT UNTIL NOW....

CHAPTER 21

JAMES COMEY
NOT ABOVE THE LAW

I swear I don't know how these dudes be getting away with it. If it's really about selective prosecution, then we got to fire the people for failing to prosecute these corrupt people. Everybody knows about these people. It's not like it's a real top-secret story. James Comey should be in jail. Like I said Harvey Weinstein should have been in jail a long time ago and now he's finally in jail. Why did it take him so long to lock him up even after Bill Cosby? I don't know, but he's locked up folks. He went to trial and he's in jail? Now people like Slippery Slopey James Comey and Lacking Candor Andrew McCabe should be in jail right next to him right folks. For a country that has a reputation for locking away people; The United States mass incarceration, we sure have a real problem about selective prosecution. I'll tell you what, there is just too much corruptness going on in our judicial system and we need to do something about it.

Everything about it just reeks. Here, we have Robert Mueller investigating the whole meddling in our election case and no wonder why James Comey has been able to slip away with it so far, it's because Mueller is his friend. Then I don't even want to

241

begin to think of why Weinstein took so long to be prosecuted. We see Bill Cosby then went through two trials and Harvey Weinstein trial didn't start for a long time. It's the same with James Comey, he then committed all these serious crimes and haven't been charged with one.

Like I say, our judicial system is really corrupt. They would give a guy 25 years to life for stealing out the store under the three strikes law, but they won't lock James Comey a serial liar and leaker up. To be honest it's not even funny. It's really a sad story and I'm disappointed to see that it has metastasized to this. In our current judicial system corruptness runs at an all-time high. We put people like James Comey above the law and you see what they do. They've been lying to judges and everyone else for years. I was just watching Comey's last interview and to be honest this dude is dumb as a box of rocks. Just everything he says is stupid.

Just the answers he gives to his questions, you're like really? I'm still trying to figure out how he made it to the be the top head FBI Director? Whoever hired him to do anything, I would hate to see what their intelligence level looks like? Everything Comey says is all over the place. I'm sorry folks, I'm just sitting here ranting and raving I know. I hope you're sitting here with me Ranting and Raving too...like these scumbags up. But seriously where is our justice and how did our judicial system get so corrupt to begin with? I don't know folks...all I can say at this point is please keep reading...

JAMES COMEY - ABSOLUTELY NO LOYALTY

DON'T FORGET ABOUT

LACKING CANDOR ANDREW MCCABE

LOCK HIM UP FOLKS
LOCK HIM TOO FOLKS

Chapter 22

JAMES COMEY
LOCK HIM UP LOCK HIM UP

I know they say, don't let one bad Apple spoil the bunch and that's Comey folks, but what's really hard to get over is when the second Apple you look into is just as rotten if not more as the first folks. That's Lacking Candor Andrew McCabe. Then the truth of the matter starts to set in. If the apples at the top are all bad, then there has to be a lot more, right? The question is how many more and how we rid the bad apples out of the bunch. So far, we got 2, and it's time that we send a stark message to the rest of them by prosecuting the two we have to date.

It would definitely show them that if the ones at the top can get prosecuted that no one is above the law. Maybe that will get them to stop their bad behavior as well, but if not prosecuting Comey and McCabe is a great step in the right direction. We talk about draining the swamp, but we won't never drain the swamp if we don't never hold anyone accountable.

In this book, I talked a lot about how paying Comey for his books in the wrong message to all the corrupt people that's been ruining our democracy. Allowing Comey to make millions off of his book tour was absolutely the wrong message for us to send

JAMES COMEY

ABSOLUTELY NO LOYALTY

By: Elliott Lew Griffin

to the world. It not only showed weakness, but it also showed that we didn't care of the wrongdoing he bestowed on our country and like I say meddling in our 2016 presidential election the way he did was by far the corruptist one in our time period not to mention the rest of them....

We have him withholding favorable evidence from judges and not to mention all the lies he's told. I know a lot of people have talked about the top-secret FBI leaking he did and I'm sure that was just the top of the iceberg. Like McCabe has even came out and said Comey was authorizing leaks in the FBI. I mean all of this comes at no surprise these days given all that we already know about Comey, but it just shows how far these people have went to try to ruin our democracy, and they're not even doing it in secret society anymore.. We have trusted them to do us a service and not only did they let us down, but they actually wound up doing us a total disservice.

I know in this book I kind of made it sound more of a joke than it was and for that I'm sorry. These people have been ruining our country for a long time and it's time that we the people stand up and hold them accountable for their actions. I know everybody asks how do we fix the problem and it's by rebuilding our sense of accountability. We see how we're rebuilding our depleted military in order to keep the bad guys in line, so we have to do that in our government as well.

They have a saying and it is: "if we don't stand for something, then will fall for anything". Here, we have to take a stand against corruption in our government or else we won't never drain the swamp. 10 years from now we will still be sitting here talking about draining the swamp and why so and so did such and such?

JAMES COMEY

ABSOLUTELY NO LOYALTY

By: Elliott Lew Griffin

Because we didn't put our foot down to end the corruption today. And that's why so and so did such and such.

We look at Comey today and see how he misled the FISA judge and withheld favorable evidence just in that one case alone. We probably should have caught him a long time ago and took his lawyer license for this kind of behavior like they did Bill Clinton. This kind of corruption is absolutely absurd at the level they were at. This kind of corruption should not be going on at the top. Nor should it be going on at the bottom either, but you think wow it really hurts when it's coming from the top. Comey and McCabe were the top guys at the FBI; an organization that we the people put in place to end criminality and corruption and they were both the corrupt criminals we were trying to stop all along.

I'll tell you what, there is no way we should be putting up with this kind of corruption. We are the greatest country in the world, and I know we not only want to keep it that way, but we actually want to make it amazing. However, the only way that we're going to do that is if we weed out all of the bad apples that are ruining the bunch. We do that and we drain the swamp.

I know it's really not your fault or mine that these guys aren't getting prosecuted, but it is our fault together because we haven't come together to end it. We live in a democracy that's ran by the people and it is supposed to be for the people and by the people, but the people we hired are really not for the people or about the people. If anything, it seems like they're against the people. Yes, we know it's our Department of Justice and Attorney General that needs to prosecute these people, but we have to start holding them accountable for their failure to do so. They have a saying and it goes: "If they're not for us then they are

JAMES COMEY

ABSOLUTELY NO LOYALTY

By: Elliott Lew Griffin

with them". Meaning if they're not on the side of promoting justice for us the American people, then they are on the side of all the criminals that's perpetuating all of the corruption.

That's why I say that if the ones in charge don't want to prosecute people like Comey and McCabe for the crimes they committed because their friends are for whatever reason, then we need to get rid of them. Or like I said we have to start prosecuting them for their failure to prosecute these people because that's really obstructing justice folks. If we want these people prosecuting and the prosecutors aren't doing it because they are allowed to do whatever they think they can do and get away with it, then we have to step in and show them they can't.

Like I said, you look up and see that bill Cosby has been prosecuted and that's a great job, but why did it take Harvey Weinstein so long to get prosecuted next? Like I say these people have been doing crimes for an awfully long time and being able to get away with it for just as long because of selective prosecution. So, my question is why aren't they prosecuting these people when they should be prosecuting these people? I mean did the prosecutors in this case except a bribe not to file charges. I'm pretty sure they have so much sexual abuse evidence against people Harvey Weinstein and everybody else in between that they should be under the jail, but then again, they're not even in jail or better yet just went to jail . It's just like with this case, Comey is not even charged with one crime out of the several that he committed. I'm serious, when you really look at it our judicial system is so corrupt on their selective prosecution scandals that it's not even funny folks. It's not even funny. These people are scumbags and they know it.

JAMES COMEY

ABSOLUTELY NO LOYALTY

By: Elliott Lew Griffin

Here, we not only have a corrupt government that's violating the law, but we also have a corrupt government that selects the ones they want to prosecute out of the people that violated the law. And that's why I say, the failure to prosecute those that violate the law is obstruction of justice. The prosecutors that don't want to prosecute people like Slippery Slopey James Comey or Lacking Candor Andrew McCabe is nothing short of obstruction of justice.

That's why I say we got to put our feet down folks. It's similar to what I told you earlier in this book about Wells Fargo the bank and how they were corruptly overcharging people. And just think if they were never caught, they would still be doing it today, with no remorse whatsoever. Please don't forget that part. (If they didn't get caught, they would still be doing it with no remorse today). If Comey was never caught and fired by Donald Trump, he would still be doing it today. Again, with no remorse. If Andrew McCabe were never caught and fired, he would still be doing it today. If Harvey Weinstein weren't prosecuted already, he would probably still be doing it today.

And the list goes on and on and on. They say people in the FBI are still leaking information and that's because no one is holding the two higher officials that they already have accountable. Here, they say someone just leaked the question Mueller planned on asking Trump if they were to ever have a sit down. I mean all of this is private investigation information that should not be leaked and again who was the leaker on the Mueller team this time. It Sure wasn't James Comey or McCabe because they were both fired before this time, so who was it other than another TOP-SECRET SERIAL LEAKER IN THE FBI, period.

JAMES COMEY

ABSOLUTELY NO LOYALTY

By: Elliott Lew Griffin

I know we could sit here and talk about this until the cows come home from the pasture but if we intend to continue to be a nation of laws, then we must start prosecuting these people to assure accountability in our society. Like they say, no one is above the law, so why aren't these people being prosecuted? I don't know folks; I just want justice myself. I know if we keep allowing corruption to occur, it's going to keep occurring. The crazy part is it's happening right in front of our eyes and we still haven't put a stop to it.

Yes, Harvey Weinstein is in jail but again don't forget that it took an awfully long time for us to get him their folks. James Comey breaks the laws right in front of our eyes and he's still not being charged. Andrew McCabe breaks the laws right in front of our eyes and he's still not being charged, so yeah okayyy. I mean this is what Hannity talks about every night on his show. Why aren't these people being charged? Then when you really stop and look at it, he's right. Why aren't these people being charged and or my question is, how are the prosecutors getting away with not charging them.

I don't know folks; I don't know. I know we have to be the difference makers in order to build our family and community ties stronger. We have to be the difference makers in holding our elected officials accountable and we have to be the difference makers by making sure justice is served on everyone participating in it. And now I know a lot of people are wonder ...how do we do that...?

WE FIND THEM, CHARGE THEM, TRY THEM AND LOCK THEM UP. JUSTICE FOLKS IS JUST THAT'S SIMPLE
JUSTICE FOLKS IS JUST THAT SIMPLE...

SLIPPERY SHADY JAMES COMEY

AND

LACKING CANDOR ANDREW MCCABE

GIVE THEM BOTH ENOUGH ROPE
AND THEY'LL HANG THEMSELVES

EPILOGUE

They always ask, what happens to the characters in the end. In this case Slippery Super Shady James Comey and Lacking Candor Andrew McCabe should eventually be charged, tried, convicted and sent to prison period. We already gave them too much rope and it's time that we pulled back on the slack. Don't worry, they're going to be the ones to hang themselves because they don't know when to quit. McCabe has already hurled the first stone by saying Comey authorized some of the leaks, so it's only a matter of time before Comey starts throwing them back. Then all we have to do from there is sit back and let their bombshell telling continue until we have enough to nab them both in the end.

I will tell you this, they always say if it's not broken then don't fix it. And that's why I'm here to tell you that our system is really broken, and we must fix it. The crazy part is it's not just bad, it's almost rotten to its core. I honestly didn't know how corrupt it was till I found myself entangled in it and then I never knew how deep the corruption went until almost 15 years had passed and I'm still in it. To say the least, real corruption in our judicial system runs deep. A lot deeper than a lot of people ever could imagine it goes and we got to fix it cause it's getting out of hand. It's not only really that bad, but it's also really that sad.... I was thinking about how I could end this book on a good note, but really folks in reality it's really all bad.

JAMES COMEY

ABSOLUTELY NO LOYALTY

By: Elliott Lew Griffin

We have allowed greed and corruption to make many of our decisions and it's gone way too far. We let it get out of hand folks. Like they say it's time that we clean house folks. It time that we cleaned up our own back yard. I will say that how we handle corruption today will determine not only our future, but our kid's future as tomorrow. So, if we don't do it for ourselves, then at least let's do it for them. One wants to know can we end corruption? I don't know, but at least we have to be on the winning end of it and right now we are losing really bad. Can we win in the end, of course we are American right? When we the American people get together, there is nothing we can't do. #Bunker-Hill. If anybody tells you otherwise, they're not American folks. They're not American period.

Well with trying to end this book on a positive note I would say "if you want to change your tomorrow it starts today". I would say that I set out with a goal in mind to write a book in a short amount of time and I actually did it, but never followed through with it until now. That's this James Comey book I wrote a while back and never fully edited it or published it.

For that I would tell you that all dreams are possible, but also, nothing comes to a sleeper but a dream. You got to put in the work if you're ever going to get anything done. And if you don't do the work, then who will right? I'm learning that myself and that's why I'm passing it on to you. Like I say I wrote this book at least a couple years ago. James Comey Absolutely No Loyalty. A $1,000,000 dollar title. And never put it out. Again, that's why I say nothing comes to a sleeper, but a dream and you must put the work in if you're ever going to get anything done. They always say, if you dream it you can achieve it, but if you have to

253

get up off your butt in order to do it. I guess in the end it's all about how bad do you want it?? How bad???

Well folks it looks like we then made it to a crossroad on this one. You are going your way and I'm going mine. Maybe we'll meet back here to do it all again another time. By the way it's nice to meet you, I'm Elliott Lew Griffin and thank you for reading my book...

JAMES COMEY - ABSOLUTELY NO LOYALTY

AND
WILL YOU PLEASE LOCK
JAMES COMEY
UP...
THANK YOU, AMERICA!

AND
THANK ME...THANK ME!

FOR WHAT?

JAMES COMEY

ABSOLUTELY NO LOYALTY

By: Elliott Lew Griffin

THE BOOK...

JAMES COMEY

ABSOLUTELY NO LOYALTY

BY ME FOLKS...

ELLIOTT LEW GRIFFIN

AKA

THE MAKE AMERICA AMAZING GUY

JAMES COMEY

ABSOLUTELY NO LOYALTY

By: Elliott Lew Griffin

OMG RIGHT!

ACKNOWLEDGMENTS

I just want to say thank you to everyone who has ever helped me along the way. I couldn't have done it without you and even if I could, it wouldn't have been as fun. To all of my family and friends, you already know you're the best family and friends in the world and that's why God gave me you.... I would name names, but the list would go on for at least quite some time, if not forever. All I can say is you know who you are, and I love you for being everything you are. Life is truly amazing and I'm glad I got to share it with you. And you with me right...otherwise just think without me you wouldn't have had no fun .... Ha-ha I just had to say that; it wouldn't be me if I didn't. OMG, got to go, TTYL (Talk To You Later)

AND PLEASE VOTE FOR ME MAKE AMERICA AMAZING FOR PRESIDENT 2024

ELLIOTT LEW GRIFFIN

THE
MAKE
AMERICA
AMAZING
GUY

For more information...please go to MAKEAMERICAAMAZING2024. COM

AND VOTE FOLKS...PLEASE DON'T FORGET TO VOTE

MAKE AMERICA AMAZING 2024

WHERE IT'S NEVER TO LATE TO BE WHAT YOU ALWAYS WANTED TO BE AND BE AMAZING AT IT!

UNLESS YOUR JAMES COMEY

OR A DO-NOTHING DEMOCRAT

JAMES COMEY

ABSOLUTELY NO LOYALTY

By: Elliott Lew Griffin

WHY?

JAMES COMEY

ABSOLUTELY NO LOYALTY

By: Elliott Lew Griffin

BECAUSE THEY'RE BOTH DONE....

THAT'S WHY!

OMG

THE
END!

BYE BYE...

JAMES COMEY

ABSOLUTELY NO LOYALTY

By: Elliott Lew Griffin

AGAIN:
ALL RIGHTS RESERVED
UNDER THE UNITED STATES
CONSTITUTION

JAMES COMEY

ABSOLUTELY NO LOYALTY

By: Elliott Lew Griffin

A LOOK:
GO GET YOUR OWN BOOK

AND OR TWO
GO TO JAIL

HOWEVER, YOU LIKE IT RIGHT?

JAMES COMEY

ABSOLUTELY NO LOYALTY

By: Elliott Lew Griffin

"TOOTLES"

Made in United States
Troutdale, OR
05/23/2024

20067843R00156